The Unique International

EASY EXCELLENT COOKING GUIDE

*A Simple Step-By-Step Method
For Beginners And Also For Accomplished Cooks*

To my dear Anne who served as
a great inspiration in encouraging me
to produce this guide.

© 1998 Serge Kaplun, Editions du Tricorne, 1201 GENÈVE
ISBN 2-8293-0176-5

Easy Excellent Cooking Guide

Written exclusively for you by
BELCAMPO

Editions du Tricorne

From the Chefs and owners of the world-famous
Auberge du Lion d'Or in Cologny / Geneva

As professionnals we perused the "Easy Excellent Cooking" with great interest. It features very appetizing recipes that one will be able to prepare quickly for an unplanned dinner with friends.

When giving cooking lessons we always make sure that the recipe is well explained, step by step, and that the timing and quantities are precisely indicated.

So we admit that the writer reached this goal, which is no easy job.

May we also encourage all beginners who enjoy cooking. Even Chefs like us have to repeat the preparation a few times before it attains the level of perfection we are seeking.

Cook also with your eyes, and the realms of cooking will be an easy game.

The contents of this book will be a source of pleasurable experience.

        Thomas Byrne   Gilles Dupont

EASY EXCELLENT COOKING GUIDE

CONTENTS

MORE THAN 120 SPECIAL CONTINENTAL AND ENGLISH RECIPES PRESENTED IN AN EASILY UNDERSTANDABLE, STEP-BY-STEP WAY. EACH RECIPE HAS BEEN GIVEN A GRADING AS FOLLOWS:

(*) = Simple   (**) = Not Difficult   (***) = Slightly More Advanced

	PAGES
INTRODUCTION	I to III
YOUR QUESTIONS ANSWERED	V
A HANDY WEIGHTS AND MEASURES GUIDE	VI
SOUPS	1 to 12
CHEESE DISHES	13 to 22
EGG DISHES	23 to 31
PASTA, PASTA SAUCES AND PIZZAS	33 to 46
RICE DISHES AND POLENTA	47 to 55
SALADS	57 to 74
VEGETABLES	75 to 91
MEAT DISHES AND POULTRY	93 to 112
FISH	113 to 123
DESSERTS	125 to 147
GLOSSARY - COOKING TERMS AND PROCESSES	149 to 153
INTERNATIONAL VOCABULARY (ENGLISH, FRENCH AND ITALIAN FOOD NAMES)	155 to 163
HOW TO COOK PASTA	165 TO 167
INDEX - ALL RECIPES IN ALPHABETICAL ORDER	169 to 179

EASY EXCELLENT COOKING GUIDE

HOW TO MASTER THE ART OF GOOD COOKING...
NOT ONLY FOR BEGINNERS BUT ALSO FOR THOSE
ALREADY SKILLED IN THE ART.

Your "Take-Off" To Easy And Excellent Cooking

INTRODUCTION TO EASY AND EXCELLENT COOKING

Dear Reader,

How to master the art of cooking and how to become an accomplished cook THE EASY WAY, using an easily understandable, step-by-step approach, written plainly and clearly!

This Guide is the key to the door for those beginners wishing to enter the field of cookery. Even those with extensive cooking experience will derive immense satisfaction by extending their knowledge in preparing many of the tempting and highly appetising dishes to be found in this guide, many of which have been passed on to me by family connections.

Let us not forget that cooking is a craft which will certainly disappear unless we continue to believe in it and practice it.

NO PREVIOUS KNOWLEDGE NEEDED TO BECOME A GREAT COOK.

Prior cooking experience is not required! The recipes in the Guide are categorised according to their degree of difficulty: degree (*) is simple, degree (**) is slightly more difficult and slightly more advanced. The objective is to bring you to degree (***) as rapidly as possible. Whilst degree (***) may seem difficult at first glance, you will take them in your stride, without difficulty, after a little practice.

TRADITIONAL EUROPEAN COOKING

The recipes given are selected from the best of my British and European cooking. There is a strong Italian flavour in many of the presentations and you will learn to make pasta the way the Italians do.

My personal view has always been that the Italian approach to meal preparation is second to none and I can think of few greater pleasures than to eat in a first-class restaurant in Florence or Rome.

PRACTICAL COOKING INFORMATION AT ITS BEST

You will discover that this is practical cooking information at its best, without an overload of sophistication. I am sure that you are like me… you like to have the essentials clearly and concisely set out. Your goal is to work on the recipe and prepare the dish in the minimum of time, without having to wade through a mass of theory. On the other hand, you want a Guide where some of the more common cookery tasks are not taken for granted, especially if you are in the beginner category. Many cookery books contain beautiful photographs of tempting dishes and I am sure that this adds colour to the presentation. BUT, you cannot eat the photos and they are not really essential when your basic task is to rapidly prepare a tasty meal. You only need the essentials.

GLOSSARY

Many of the essential culinary terms are listed and explained in this section.

INTERNATIONAL VOCABULARY

French and Italian food names are listed against the English equivalent in the International Vocabulary Section.

I am sure you will enjoy this Guide as much as I did in preparing it.

BELCAMPO
(Douglas F. Schofield)

EASY EXCELLENT COOKING GUIDE

WHY I DECIDED TO WRITE "EASY EXCELLENT COOKING".

The need to be able to cook becomes a reality when we have to face up to certain specific events in our lives. Some of us prefer not to be involved until there is really no other choice and then we find that we need to learn fast.

Amongst a host of other circumstances., there are two distinct periods when we are faced with the task of learning how to cook, with the alternative of just not eating. Starting with our student days, or first employment, usually from the age of about 18 onwards, we are immediately confronted with this problem (if not living at home). One is driven to learn to cook rather than relying on the more expensive solutions of living on snacks or eating in restaurants.

The second category concerns mainly persons like myself who, apart from the odd cup of tea, boiled egg or prepared dish, very successfully avoided what was considered both a boring and unnecessary occupation. Cooking for myself was unheard of and, if my wife was away for some reason or another, it would be straight to the restaurant.

Suddenly, the axe dropped and I was faced with the necessity of preparing an evening meal. Finding an easy recipe would be "a piece of cake", I said to myself. My confidence proved to be entirely unjustified when I pored over numerous cookery books, only to find that I could not understand one word. I discovered an extraordinary vocabulary intended for the chosen few but incomprehensible to beginners. I was reminded of the first time that I read a book on currency futures. "Fold your dollops into the stock" was beyond me!

I happened to be giving a series of lectures at a university in Switzerland during this period. Between lectures, I raised with the students the problem of attempting to find clear, precise step-by-step recipes and I was surprised to find that they all agreed with me. They were experiencing the same difficulties in finding easily understandable recipes for beginners. The first seed was planted, now that I realised that I was not alone.

From that moment on, I decided to unravel the secrets of simple, excellent cooking and I found myself in a new, enthralling universe. How much I regret now that I did not start sooner!

Thus it was that I decided to re-write many of the recipes used by my wife and her family and to present many of these superb dishes, with easy-to-understand explanations, intended for use by the young, the not-so-young, in fact by budding cooks of all ages.

EASY EXCELLENT COOKING GUIDE

What are the preparation and cooking times - The recipes are for how many persons? - Types of utensils required?

(Q) Preparation and cooking times - how exact are the times which are given with each recipe?
(A) Time factors indicated will obviously differ according to the degree of expertise of the person who is cooking. A "professional" will need less time than the times indicated.
My preparation time does include the washing of the utensils as you progress. I find it more efficient to wash up as one proceeds, thereby keeping all working space clear and tidy. Others often believe in doing the washing-up at the end of the meal, in which case the working space often resembles a "battle-field".
Another important point - try and assemble, prior to starting, all the ingredients and cooking utensils which you are going to need.

(Q) The recipes are for what number of persons?
(A) This is indicated at the top of each recipe page. It is nice to have recipes available for 6, 8 and 10 persons, but let us face reality - most of our cooking will involve 2 to 4 persons, and many times we are cooking just for number one… ourselves.

(Q) What type of utensils are needed?
(A) These are all standard kitchen utensils. An elaborate listing of equipment is not necessarily helpful. We usually try to make do with what we have rather than chasing out to buy a new kitchen appliance each time a book says we require such an instrument.

KNOW YOUR WEIGHTS AND MEASURES

To ensure success, you should try and keep to the quantities and measures recommended below.

Conversions of Weights, Measures and Temperatures

Metric	British	Metric	British
10/15g	1/2 oz	1/2 dl	2 fl oz (4 tbspn)
20/25g	1 oz	3/4 dl	3 fl oz
50g	2 oz	1 dl	4 fl oz
75g	3 oz	1 1/2 dl	1/4 pint
100g	4 oz	1 3/4 dl	6 fl oz
150g	5 oz	2 dl	7 fl oz
175g	6 oz	2 1/2 dl	8 fl oz
200g	7 oz	3 dl	1/2 pint
225g	8 oz	4 dl	14 fl oz
250g	9 oz	4 1/2 dl	3/4 pint
300g	11 oz	5 dl	18 fl oz
350g	12 oz	6 dl	1 pint
375g	13 oz	7 dl	1 pint 4 fl oz
400g	14 oz	8 dl	1 pint 8 fl oz
450g	1 lb	9 dl	1 1/2 pints
500g	1 lb 2oz	1 litre	1 3/4 pints
600g	1 1/4 lbs		
700g	1 1/2 lbs	Conversion:	1 litre
800g	1 3/4 lbs		= 1.76 pints
900g	2 lbs		

Conversion: 1 kilogram = 2.205 lbs

Note: The conversions between metric and British weights and measures are rounded off to make easier working quantities. The American pint differs inasmuch as it equals 16 fl oz, instead of 20 fl oz under the British system.

TEMPERATURES °C		°F	Gas Mark
Very slow oven	120-140	250-275	0.25-0.5
Slow	150-160	300-325	1-2
Moderate	180-190	350-375	3-5
Hot	200-220	400-425	6-7
Very hot	230-250	450-475	8-9

EASY EXCELLENT COOKING GUIDE

SOUPS

British and European Cooking at its Best

Preparation time: 15 minutes
Cooking time: 55 minutes

CELERY SOUP (**)

2 PERSONS
450 G/1 LB CELERIAC (TURNIP-ROOTED TYPE OF CELERY)
1 DL/4 FL OZ MILK
1 BROTH CUBE
3 TABLESPOONS YOGHURT (NATURAL)
1 EGG YOLK
GARLIC ⎫
ONION ⎬ SPRINKLING OF EACH (DRY)
OREGANO ⎭
1 1/4 LITRES / 2 1/4 PINTS WATER
SALT AND PEPPER

1) Wash and peel the celeriac. Cut into small pieces (for quicker cooking). Place in 3/4 litres/1 1/4 pints salted water, cook for 40 minutes - use a lid.

2) When the celeriac is cooked (soft and tender) strain, cool and pass through a food mill to make a purée.

3) Separately, in a glass or small mixing bowl, blend an egg yolk with 3 tablespoons of yoghurt (natural) and mix well.

4) Bring 1/2 litre/approx.1 pint water to a boil, add the purée and the broth cube, garlic, onion, pepper and oregano. Retain on a low heat for a few minutes; stir gently, add the milk, and finally pour in the yoghurt and egg yolk mixture, continuing to stir.

Your soup is now ready for serving.

Note: This is one of my favourite soups.

Preparation time: 15 minutes
Cooking time: 45 minutes

FENNEL SOUP (**)

2 OR 3 PERSONS
600 G/1 1/4 LB FENNELS (2 OR 3 MEDIUM SIZE FENNELS)
1 BROTH CUBE (IF NO STOCK AVAILABLE)
1 1/2 DL/1/4 PINT MILK
3 TABLESPOONS YOGHURT (NATURAL)
1 EGG YOLK
GARLIC DRY ⎫
ONION " ⎬ JUST A SPRINKLE OF EACH
CELERY SALT " ⎬
OREGANO " ⎭
1 1/4 LITRES/2 1/4 PINTS WATER
SALT AND BLACK PEPPER

1) Wash the fennels, cut away all stalks, sprigs and other tough leaves, leaving just the bulbs. Cut up the bulbs into small slices (so that they cook quicker) and wash again.

2) Place the fennels in 3/4 litre of salted water, and cook for 30 minutes - cover the saucepan with a lid. Cook on a low heat until the fennels are tender.

3) After 30 minutes, strain the fennels, cool, pass them through a food mill (sieve) to produce a purée.

4) Now return to your saucepan again and bring 1/2 litre/1 pint water to a boil, add the broth cube; add the dry garlic, onion, celery salt, oregano and pepper along with the fennel purée (3). Reduce the heat to very low (simmer) for 5 minutes, stir gently but well.

5) Separately, mix the egg yolk with 3 tbsp yoghurt.

6) Now add the milk to the soup; continue to stir on a low heat, and finally pour in the egg/yoghurt mixture, continuing to stir.

Voilà, your Fennel Soup is now ready for serving.

Preparation time: 10 minutes
Cooking time: 45 minutes

GARLIC SOUP (*)

3 TO 4 PERSONS
3 LARGE CLOVES GARLIC, FINELY CHOPPED
2 MEAT BROTH CUBES, OR STOCK
3 EGG YOLKS
4 TABLESPOONS OLIVE OIL
1 TABLESPOON FRESH THYME
SAGE LEAVES, FINELY CHOPPED (APPROX. 2 TABLESPOONS WHEN CHOPPED)
1 BAY-LEAF
2 CLOVES
PINCH OF SAFFRON
BUNCH PARSLEY, FINELY CHOPPED
1 LITRE/1 3/4 PINTS WATER
CELERY SALT, OR COOKING SALT
BLACK PEPPER

1) Bring the water to a boil, add the broth cubes, and then the garlic. With the water continuing to boil add the thyme, sage, laurel, cloves, saffron, celery salt, pinch of pepper.

2) After 2 to 3 minutes lower the heat and allow to simmer for 30 minutes.

3) Beat the egg yokes (with a whisk) in a separate bowl and very gradually add the olive oil continuing to whisk so that the end result is a creamy substance.

4) After 30 minutes add the parsley and stir; now remove the soup from the heat and mix in the egg substance, beating with a whisk.

Do not strain the soup, and serve nice and hot.

Preparation time: 10 minutes
Cooking time: 35 minutes

GREEN PEA SOUP (*)

2 PERSONS
600 G/1 1/4 LB GREEN PEAS
1/2 BROTH CUBE
1 DL/4 FL OZ MILK
3 MINT LEAVES, FINELY CHOPPED
1 CLOVE GARLIC, FINELY CHOPPED
1 SMALL ONION, FINELY CHOPPED
PINCH OF SALT (1/4 TEASPOON)
PEPPER

1) Remove the peas from the pods, wash the peas, and cook in 1 litre/1 3/4 pints water in which you have first added 1/2 of a broth cube and the finely chopped mint leaves. Cover the saucepan. Cooking time 15 to 20 minutes.

2) The liquid, or broth, in which you have cooked the peas is the basis for the soup, so retain and set aside. Strain the peas and place them in a food mill or sieve to make a purée. Stir this purée into the broth.

3) Now pour 1 dl/4 fl oz milk into the broth, add the chopped garlic and onion, add a little pepper and salt, and allow to just simmer for 10 minutes, stirring occasionally.

Preparation time: 10 minutes
Cooking time: 50 minutes

LENTIL SOUP (*)

2 PERSONS
6 TABLESPOONS (BROWN) LENTILS (SOAKED)
10 G/ 1/2 OZ BUTTER
1 TABLESPOON PLAIN WHITE FLOUR
10 G/ 1/2 OZ PARSLEY, FINELY CHOPPED
FRESH THYME (APPROX. 6 SPRIGS)
2 SMALL ONIONS, FINELY CHOPPED
1/2 CLOVE GARLIC, FINELY CHOPPED
2 RASHERS OF BACON, DICED
1 LITRE/1 3/4 PINTS WATER
1 BROTH CUBE (MEAT)
1 DL/4 FL OZ MILK
CELERY SALT OR COOKING SALT
"HERBES DE PROVENCE" (MIXED HERBS)
BLACK PEPPER

If there is any doubt, soak the lentils overnight (soaking instructions are usually indicated on the wrapper together with the cooking time).

1) Bring the water to a boil and add the broth cube.

2) Separately, using a large pan, melt the butter. Add the finely chopped onions, garlic, parsley and bacon (diced) stir and sauté for a minute or two. Now slowly pour all the broth into the pan, adding the flour as you pour. Stir.

3) Add the lentils, a pinch of pepper and salt, the "herbes de provence" and cover with a lid. Cook on a medium to low heat for 40 minutes. Occasionally taste the lentils to see if they are nice and soft, at which time add your milk, stir well, add the thyme. Serve hot. If the lentils remain hard continue to cook for another 15 to 20 minutes.

Note: 6 tablespoons of lentils are equal to 125 g/4 1/2 oz - if you wish to have a thicker soup increase the quantity of lentils to 150 g/5 oz (7 to 8 tablespoons).

Preparation time: 20 minutes
Cooking time: 1 hr. 50 minutes

MINESTRONE (***) (A thick vegetable soup containing also rice or pasta)

3 TO 4 PERSONS
100 G/4 OZ HARICOT BEANS ("SOISSONS") SOAKED OVERNIGHT, OR AT LEAST FOR 12 HOURS
100 G/4 OZ BACON OR PANCETTA, CUT INTO SMALL SQUARES (DICED)
1-2 SMALL ONIONS, FINELY CHOPPED
1-2 CLOVES GARLIC, " "
350 G/12 OZ POTATOES, CARROTS, STEMS OF CELERY (2 POTATOES, 2 CARROTS, 2 STEMS CELERY) ALL DICED
100 G/4 OZ SMALL CRISP CABBAGE, FINELY CHOPPED
300 G/11 OZ TOMATOES, PEELED AND CRUSHED
100 G/4 OZ RICE   20 G/1 OZ BUTTER
FRESH BASIL AND PARSLEY, FINELY CHOPPED
2 TABLESPOONS OLIVE OIL   SALT & PEPPER
GRATED CHEESE   1 BROTH CUBE, OR STOCK

1) First cook the beans in 1 1/2 litres/2 1/2 pints water, 3/4 tablespoon salt, for 30 to 40 minutes, or even longer, as indicated on the packing - refer to the total cooking time on the packing, but deduct one hour (because you are going to continue cooking the beans together with all the other vegetables for one hour under (3) below). Remove from the heat and retain in the water.

2) Using a large saucepan, sauté the onions and garlic, bacon (or pancetta) in butter for 1 to 2 minutes.

3) Add the vegetables (potatoes, carrots, celery) having first peeled the potatoes, scraped the carrots, sliced the celery, all washed and diced. Add one broth cube (if no stock). Add the beans in their water (1). Check water to ensure that the vegetables are just covered, and add water as necessary. Stir. Cook on a medium to low heat for one hour.

4) Cabbage preparation: remove outer leaves, cut into four portions after first removing the woody core and any stalks, wash, chop on a board (chop fine). Add the cabbage along with the tomatoes (which have first been peeled and crushed). Add the rice, basil, parsley, pepper. All these items under (4) should be added 20 minutes before the end (i.e. 40 minutes after commencing (3) Step up the heat for a few minutes, then reduce to a low boil and continue cooking for the remaining 20 minutes. Add 2 tablespoons olive oil just before removing from the heat and serving. Use grated cheese according to taste.

Note: Minestrone is really not complicated but it does take time. The cabbage can be replaced with French green beans.

Preparation time: 8 minutes
Cooking time: 10 minutes
(XF = Extra-fast)

THICK TOMATO SOUP (*)

(Fr. Velouté de Tomate)

2 TO 3 PERSONS
1 TIN OF CONDENSED TOMATO SOUP, SUCH AS CAMPBELL'S "VELOUTÉ DE TOMATE" (APPROX. 300 G/11 OZ)
1 EGG, HARD-BOILED, CHOPPED INTO THIN SLICES
1/2 GLASS SHERRY, OR MARSALA
3 TABLESPOONS PARSLEY, OR BASIL, MINCED
BLACK PEPPER AND SALT

1) Empty the contents of the tin into a saucepan, add the same quantity of water, stir. Instead of water you can add the equivalent quantity in milk or cream.

2) Continue to stir slowly and bring the soup to a boil. As soon as it starts to boil, remove immediately, add the boiled egg slices, the minced parsley or basil, the Sherry or Marsala, a little black pepper and salt. Mix and stir.

Serve hot.

The above solution for making tomato soup is about the most simple and fast, however, if you are in a great hurry then the ready-made variety of soups in powder form come in handy: as an example, take a Chervil herb soup (70 g. approx.) prepare as per instructions. Whenever possible replace 1 dl (about a small glass) of water with milk, and add such ingredients as Worcester sauce, dry rosemary, garlic, celery salt, pepper, etc.

Preparation time: 12 minutes
Cooking time: 40 minutes

TOMATO SOUP (*)

2 TO 3 PERSONS
500 G/1 LB 2 OZ TOMATOES
2 CLOVES GARLIC, MINCED
1 CARROT, MINCED
1 SMALL ONION, MINCED
1 CELERY, MINCED
2 TABLESPOONS PARSLEY. MINCED
15 G/1/2 OZ FLOUR
1 1/2 DL/1/4 PINT MILK
6 DL/1 PINT CHICKEN BROTH (1 BROTH CUBE)
3 TABLESPOONS OIL (SUNFLOWER)
2 TABLESPOONS FRESH BASIL (REDUCE TO SMALL LEAVES)
SALT AND BLACK PEPPER

1) Wash and prepare the carrot, celery, parsley, onion and garlic. Mince all these ingredients (use a mincer).

2) Wash the tomatoes and place them in boiling water for 1 or 2 minutes - peel off the skins.

3) Line a pan with oil - heat; sauté the ingredients which you have prepared under (1) above -gradually pour in the hot broth (the broth is prepared separately).

4) Add the peeled tomatoes and crush them down using a wooden spoon. Cook over a medium heat for 30 minutes (cover) then pass everything through a sieve or food mill making a purée. Return to the same pan - add pepper and salt, (a pinch only).

5) Mix your flour thoroughly with a little milk (avoid lumps forming - if necessary beat with a mixer). Add this to the soup. Now add the remainder of the milk. Re-heat the soup until it thickens, and continue to stir. Add the small basil leaves. Serve hot.

Preparation time: 15 minutes
Cooking time: 45 minutes

VEGETABLE SOUP (**)

2 PERSONS (AS A MAIN DISH, OR FOR 4 AS A STARTER)
1 SMALL CELERIAC
4 MEDIUM POTATOES
3 CARROTS
1 MEAT BROTH CUBE (IF NO MEAT STOCK AVAILABLE)
GARLIC ⎫
⎬ 1/2 TEASPOON OF EACH, DRY
ONION ⎭
WORCESTER SAUCE [2 GOOD SHAKES]
BLACK PEPPER
PINCH OF CELERY SALT (OPTIONAL)
1 TABLESPOON COOKING SALT
FRESH OREGANO, OR DRY
1 TABLESPOON OLIVE OIL

1) Wash the vegetables thoroughly before peeling. Reduce to small pieces for easy cooking. Wash again before cooking in salted water for 30 minutes (potatoes take less time to cook so remove when cooked and continue cooking the other vegetables).

2) When all the vegetables are cooked, place them in a bowl and allow to cool. Now pass all the vegetables through a food mill or sieve to produce a purée. Transfer this purée to a clean saucepan.

3) Add 1/2 litre/1 pint water to the pan (with the purée). Now add the meat broth cube, the garlic, onion, pepper, a little celery salt, oregano, and Worcester sauce. Continue to mix and stir on a low boil. Add more water as required so that the top of the liquid remains just above the ingredients in the pan.

4) Continue to stir. After 10 minutes taste your soup and it should be really excellent - for the professional touch add a tablespoon of olive oil. Continue to stir, switch off, and serve hot.

Preparation time: 20-25 minutes

GAZPACHO (*)
(cold vegetable soup)

> 4 TO 6 PERSONS
> 600 G/1 1/4 LB RIPE TOMATOES (ABOUT 6 MEDIUM TOMATOES)
> 1 CUCUMBER
> 1 GREEN PEPPER
> 150 G/5 OZ BREAD, SLIGHTLY HARD
> 1/2 GLASS OLIVE OIL
> 2 TABLESPOONS VINEGAR
> 2 DL/1/2 PINT WATER
> 3 CLOVES GARLIC, CRUSHED
> 1 TEASPOON SALT

1) Take about 100 g/4 oz bread crumbs and mix with the olive oil (using a large bowl). Mince or crush the garlic, mix with the bread and olive oil. After mixing well, set aside.

2) Proceed to deseed and wash the peppers (refer Page 82). Peel, deseed and wash the cucumber. Dice both the peppers and cucumber (cut into small cubes).

   Wash the tomatoes and remove their skins (put the tomatoes into boiling hot water for one minute so as to easily remove the skins). Remove the hard cores and deseed - cut into small parts.

3) Add two-thirds of each of the peppers, cucumber and tomatoes (already diced) to the bowl containing the bread, olive oil and garlic. Now add the vinegar, salt and mix all the contents well.
   Pass all the contents through a sieve to liquidise all the ingredients. Once liquidised, dilute with 3 dl/1/2 pint of water, according to taste and also depending on the number of servings. Stir well before serving. I usually add a few ice cubes before putting the gazpacho into the refrigerator.

4) Garnish - Don't overlook the garnish. The remaining diced peppers, cucumber, and tomatoes together with the remaining bread (cut the bread into small cubes) should be put on side-plates.

EASY EXCELLENT COOKING GUIDE

CHEESE DISHES

BRITISH AND EUROPEAN COOKING AT ITS BEST

Preparation time: 7 minutes
Cooking time: 15 minutes

CROÛTE AU FROMAGE AVEC LARD OU JAMBON (*)

Cheese with bacon or ham, on croûtes of fried bread

2 PERSONS
280 G/10 OZ GRUYÈRE CHEESE, CUT INTO SLICES SO THAT THERE ARE 3 TO 4 FOR EACH SLICE OF BREAD
4 SLICES OF BACON
4 LARGE SLICES OF BREAD (NOT TOO THICK)
4 TABLESPOONS OIL (SUNFLOWER)
15 G/ 1/2 OZ BUTTER
PAPRIKA OR PEPPER

1) Line a large, shallow, non-stick frying pan with oil, and heat.

   Place the bread into the hot oil and brown on one side only (reduce the heat if there is a risk of burning the bread).

2) Remove the bread (when brown on one side) and turn the bread slices so that the brown side is on top. Add the cheese slices on top of the bread (3 to 4 cheese parts to each slice of bread). Sprinkle a little paprika or pepper over the cheese surfaces.

3) Quickly dip the bacon into the pan (which you have just used) and fry for 1 minutes. Remove and add on top of the cheese.

4) Remove any surplus oil from the pan. Melt a little butter in the same pan. Place the bread slices (with the cheese and bacon) into the pan. Cover the pan with a lid. Turn up the heat slowly and then start reducing.

   Occasionally check to see if the cheese is melting (and that the bread is not burning).

   When the cheese has nicely melted, your "croûtes" are done.

   Depending on the heat control, the cheese melting process should take from 5 to 10 minutes. With a low heat (with less risk of burning the bread) you will require about 7 to 10 minutes.

Preparation time: 15 minutes
Cooking time: 35 minutes

SAVOURY CHEESE FLAN (***)

2 TO 3 PERSONS (AS A MAIN DISH, OR 4 PERSONS IF THE CHEESE FLAN IS A STARTER)
275G/10 OZ PASTRY FOR BAKING
400G/14 OZ CHEESE (1/2 GRUYÈRE 1/2 VACHERIN DE FRIBOURG)
2 EGGS
3 TO 4 DL/BETWEEN 1/2 & 3/4 PINT MILK
1 TEASPOON NUTMEG
1/2 TEASPOON GARLIC POWDER
FRESH THYME

In this recipe we are going to use ready-made dough/pastry, pre-rolled and cut to approx. size of our baking tray (diameter approx. 30 cm). There are various qualities of pastry; better to select one suitable for non-sweet contents (shortcrust or puff pastry/pâte feuilletée).

1) Prepare the pastry in the quantity required to cover a round shallow ovenproof baking tray (pastry should also cover the sides of the tray) After the pastry is set in the tray use a fork to make holes in the pastry (to avoid it rising).

2) Grate the cheese and place the grated cheese into a large bowl. Crack open two eggs and mix complete with the cheese. Pour the milk into the bowl with the cheese and eggs, but judge the quantity of milk so as to avoid the mixture becoming too liquid (this is the key to having a first class cheese flan). If you like nutmeg taste use a good measure, plus a little garlic powder (not essential). Add the thyme.
Stir the contents of the bowl well, again making sure that the mixture is not too liquid - if too liquid add more grated cheese.

3) Pre-heat the oven to 200°C/400°F/Gas Mark 6 for 10 minutes.

4) Pour the contents of the bowl into the tray, and place the tray into the oven.

5) Cooking time approx. 25 minutes at 180°C/350°F/Gas Mark 4 until the flan becomes a nice brown colour

Notes: Before spreading the pastry into the baking tray cover the inside of the tray with little butter so it is well greased (to avoid sticking). With pre-rolled pastry you usually get grease paper which means we do not have to grease the tray.
Grating: grating cheese is much faster with a mechanical grater.

Preparation time: 10 minutes
Cooking time: 25 minutes

SAVOURY TOMATOES WITH CHEESE (**)

2 OR 3 PERSONS
SERVE AS A STARTER, OR AS A SMALL MAIN DISH WITH A GREEN SALAD.
3 LARGE, OR 5 SMALL TOMATOES (APPROX.500 G/1 LB 2 OZ)
75 G/3 OZ BACON, FINELY CHOPPED OR DICED
25 G/1 OZ ONIONS, MINCED
1 CLOVE GARLIC, MINCED
1/2 BUNCH PARSLEY, MINCED
4 TABLESPOONS GRATED CHEESE
2 TABLESPOONS OIL (SUNFLOWER)
SPRINKLE OF "HERBES DE PROVENCE" (MIXED DRY HERBS)

1) Wash the tomatoes. Make a large round hole at the top of each tomato (ideal instrument is a grapefruit knife). Remove the contents with a spoon (go just deep enough to make space for a portion of stuffing - maximum would equal approx. 1/2 the inside of the tomato).

2) First insert a portion of the bacon as a bottom-layer of stuffing in each tomato. Mix the remaining bacon together with the minced onion, garlic and parsley. Fill the tomatoes with this mixture, press down, and add the grated cheese on top. Finally, add a sprinkling of mixed dry herbs ("herbes de Provence") over the grated cheese.

3) Place the tomatoes upright (grated cheese on top) in an ovenproof dish (add a little oil to the dish so that the tomatoes do not stick) and cook in a preheated oven for 20 minutes at 180°C/350°F/Gas Mark 4.

Note: Any surplus tomato or ingredients can be placed in a salad bowl and used as a basis for a green salad.

Preparation time: 10-15 minutes
Cooking time: 1 hr.

CHEESE SOUFFLE (***)

"Soufflé au Fromage"

> **2 TO 3 PERSONS**
> **300 G/11 OZ CHEESE, GRATED (USE 150 G/5 OZ GRUYÈRE,**
> **150 G/5 OZ EMMENTHAL, OR TILSIT)**
> **60 G/2 1/2 OZ PLAIN WHITE FLOUR**
> **10 G/1/2 OZ BUTTER**
> **1/2 LITRE/1 PINT MILK**
> **1/2 TEASPOON PAPRIKA**
> **4 EGGS**
> **COOKING SALT**
> **BLACK PEPPER**

1) Using a medium heat, pour the milk slowly into the saucepan mixing it with the flour. Continue to stir to obtain a thickish substance like cream, but not too solid. Add a pinch of salt. Remove the pan from the heat and allow to cool for 10 minutes.

2) Add the paprika and grated cheese and mix slowly. Crack open the eggs and separate the whites and yolks. Add the yolks to the saucepan and again mix slowly. Season with salt and pepper. Whisk the egg whites until stiff and transfer to the saucepan, continuing to mix slowly (egg whites give your soufflé the lift).

3) Pour all the contents of the saucepan into an ovenproof dish (which you have greased beforehand with a little butter). Preheat the oven, and bake the soufflé for 45 minutes at 180°C/350°F/Gas Mark 4.

Preparation time: 5 minutes
Cooking time: 10-15 minutes

WELSH RABBIT (**)

(Welsh Rarebit)

2 OR 4 PERSONS (AS A MAIN DISH FOR 2, AND AS A STARTER OR SAVOURY FOR FOUR PERSONS)
4 SLICES OF TOAST
150G/5 OZ CHEDDAR CHEESE, GRATED (APPROX. 7 TO 8 TABLESPOONS)
3 TO 4 TABLESPOONS MILK
4 TEASPOONS MARGARINE OR BUTTER
PEPPER AND SALT

Really an easy dish, but you are still juggling with three operations almost at the same time; any lack of attention and the bread will be burnt.

1) Start by slowly toasting four slices of bread, and keep hot.

2) Heat a shallow grease-proof pan and melt the margarine or butter. Add your grated Cheddar cheese into the pan, then the milk, and a little pepper and salt. Stir well, and when nice and liquid pour slowly on to the slices of toast.

3) Now place the 4 slices under a pre-heated grill (preheated for five minutes) counting approx. two to three minutes, at 220°C/425°F/Gas Mark 7.

Serve hot.

N.B. If in a real hurry, forget the last operation consisting of placing the toast under the grill. Even without the grill this little dish tastes good, but the grill makes it excellent.

Preparation time: 5-10 minutes
Cooking time: 10-15 minutes

BÉCHAMEL SAUCE (*)

2 TO 6 PERSONS (DEPENDING ON APPLICATION - IF USED FOR A GRATIN = 2 TO 4 PERSONS: AS A SAUCE TO ACCOMPANY FISH OR VEGETABLES = 6 PERSONS)
40 G/2 OZ FLOUR
40 G/2 OZ BUTTER
3 DL/1/2 PINT FRESH MILK
1 DL/4 FL OZ WATER (COLD)
1 TO 2 TEASPOONS SALT
1/2 TO 3/4 TEASPOON PEPPER
1/2 TEASPOON NUTMEG

1) Commence by bringing the milk to a boil. Remove the milk and let it cool slightly before adding the cold water (mix the water with the milk). Set aside.

2) Take a clean saucepan - melt the butter over a medium heat. Now start reducing the heat and add the flour slowly - stir to get a smooth cream (you are now using a low heat).
Continuing to stir over a low heat, pour all the milk and water into the butter/flour mixture, and continue to stir slowly.

3) Stir slowly until a thickish cream develops. Now step up the heat gradually to reach boiling, at which time quickly add the salt, pepper, nutmeg and remove from the heat immediately - continue to stir. Return to a very low heat and your Béchamel is ready!
Just a question of heat control, otherwise quite easy to make.

Variation - an important variation which I use when making a gratin:

Same ingredients as above, but add

1 EGG YOLK
3 TABLESPOONS GRATED CHEESE
2 TABLESPOONS BREADCRUMBS

Beat the egg yolk and mix with the grated cheese; add the egg and grated cheese mixture just as you remove from the heat [in 3 above] after having added the salt, pepper, and nutmeg.

The breadcrumbs are sprinkled over the surface before placing your gratin in the oven.

Preparation time: 25 minutes
Cooking time: 25 minutes

CHEESE BISCUITS (**)

(Fr. Galettes au fromage)

>   MAKES 18 TO 20
>   75 G/3 OZ CHEDDAR CHEESE, FINELY GRATED
>   50 G/2 OZ BUTTER
>   75 G/3 OZ PLAIN FLOUR
>   1 EGG YOLK, BEATEN
>   1/2 A SMALL GLASS OF SINGLE CREAM
>   1/2 LEMON JUICE
>   CAYENNE, WHITE PEPPER AND SALT
>   PLUS A LITTLE BUTTER FOR GREASING THE BAKING TRAY

1) Use a large mixing bowl. Add the flour to the bowl. Using your fingertips, rub in small pieces of butter. Now add the cheese. Season with cayenne, pepper and salt.

2) Pour in the egg yoke. Mix the ingredients with your floured hands. Add the lemon juice and a small drop of cream, and continue mixing until you have a stiff dough.

3) Flour your board and roll out the dough to approx. 1/2 cm/ 1/4" thickness. Stamp into small rounds approx. 4 cm/1 3/4" diameter using a special cutting knife or using the rim of a small glass.

4) Prick the rounds with a fork before placing them on a baking tray (which you have previously greased with a little butter). Pre-heat the oven for 10 minutes. Insert your baking tray or sheet with the rounds into the oven, and bake for 10 to 15 minutes at 180°C/350°/Gas Mark 4 until slightly brown.

When cool, place the biscuits/galettes into an air-tight tin until needed, although they are best when slightly warm.

Preparation time: 10 minutes
Cooking time: 5 minutes

CHEESE AND EGG RELISH (*)

2 PERSONS (AS A STARTER OR SNACK)
7 TABLESPOONS GRUYÈRE CHEESE, GRATED
2 EGGS
4 LARGE SLICES OF BREAD (FOR TOASTING)
1 TABLESPOON PLAIN FLOUR
4 TABLESPOONS SINGLE CREAM
3 TABLESPOONS MILK
15 G/1/2 OZ BUTTER
SALT AND PEPPER

1) Use a large mixing or salad bowl. Mix 1 tablespoon cream with the flour (in the bowl). Add the 2 eggs and beat.

2) Separately, mix all the milk with the remainder of the cream. Pour this into the bowl, and continue to beat (using a fork, or whip with a whisk). Add a little salt and pepper.
Lastly, add the grated cheese. Continue to beat until you have almost a thickish liquid.

3) Use a shallow, frying pan. Put in your butter and let it melt over a medium heat. Now pour in your mixture (2), slightly reducing the heat. Cooking time is 2 to 3 minutes only. The mixture should become lumpy, not liquid (use a wooden spoon to control the mixture bringing it gradually into the centre of the pan).

4) In the meantime, toast your bread. Using a largish serving spatula, space the mixture evenly over the toasted bread slices, and serve hot.

Note: This dish is quick and easy to prepare

EASY EXCELLENT COOKING GUIDE

EGG DISHES

BRITISH AND EUROPEAN COOKING AT ITS BEST

Preparation time: 10 minutes
Cooking time: 50 minutes

ARTICHOKE OMELETTE (**)

2 PERSONS
1 LARGE, OR 2 OR 3 SMALL ARTICHOKES
4 EGGS
3 TABLESPOONS GRATED CHEESE, PARMESAN
1/2 DL/2 FL OZ MILK
20 G/1 OZ BUTTER
2 TABLESPOONS OIL (SUNFLOWER)
1/2 TABLESPOON PLAIN FLOUR
BLACK PEPPER AND SALT

1) Boil the artichoke in salted water for 45 minutes (boiling time depends on the size - smaller artichokes take less cooking time). If you use a pressure pan, count 15 minutes.

2) The artichoke will become soft after cooking and the leaves easy to detach. Let it chill. Remove the hairy choke (beard) and throw away. Cut out the heart and reduce to small pieces. Remove the flesh from the leaves (scrape).
Place the heart and flesh into a large flat sauté pan with a thin layer of oil. Heat, and sauté the contents of the pan for a few minutes, adding a pinch of salt.

3) Crack open 4 eggs and pour them into a bowl for mixing; beat well. Pour in the artichoke mixture. Continue to mix and stir. Pour 1/2 dl/ 2 fl oz milk into the bowl, beat well. Add the flour and continue beating. Add 3 tablespoons grated cheese, beat and stir. Add salt and black pepper.

Line a large flat non-stick pan with a thin layer of oil, medium heat, and when hot pour in the contents of the mixing bowl.

4) Proceed as for a simple omelette explained on page 26 steps 3/4/5

Preparation time: 5-10 minutes
Cooking time: 10 minutes

CHEESE OMELETTE WITH PARSLEY (*)

2 PERSONS
4 EGGS
3 TABLESPOONS GRATED CHEESE
1/2 DL/2 FL OZ MILK
20 G/1 OZ BUTTER
1 TABLESPOON OIL (SUNFLOWER)
PARSLEY, FINELY CHOPPED
SALT AND BLACK PEPPER

1) Crack open the eggs. Pour them into a mixing bowl and beat vigorously. Add the milk, continue to beat and stir. Now add the grated cheese, mix and stir. Add the parsley, salt and pepper, continue to stir.

2) Pour one or two tablespoons oil into a wide flat pan, and heat. When hot, pour the contents of the bowl into the pan (make sure the mixture is spread out evenly to cover the entire pan). Reduce the heat.

3) Press the mixture down into the pan so that it cooks and becomes more solid (no longer liquid, but not too solid).
To avoid having the underside burnt allow some of the egg liquid to run underneath (so that all the omelette cooks).

4) Transfer the contents of the pan to a large plate (simply slide the mixture on to a plate).
Place a second similar plate on top, turn the plates upside down (reverse the omelette).

5) Place butter into your pan, heat. Slide the mixture back into the pan, control heat, do not let the mixture burn. Flatten the mixture into the pan. Try and keep the omelette moist and slightly juicy.

Serve hot with a green salad.

Note: The tricky part is reversing the egg mixture, keeping the omelette moist and juicy (not dry) and controlling the heat.

Preparation time: 10 minutes
Cooking time: 20 minutes

COURGETTE OMELETTE (**)

2 PERSONS
4 EGGS
2 SMALL COURGETTES ("ZUCCHINI")
3 TABLESPOONS GRATED CHEESE (PARMESAN)
1/2 DL/2 FL OZ MILK 3 TABLESPOONS OIL (SUNFLOWER)
20 G/1 OZ BUTTER
1/2 CLOVE GARLIC, FINELY CHOPPED
PARSLEY, FINELY CHOPPED
1/2 TEASPOON SALT AND A PINCH OF PEPPER

1) Wash the courgettes. Cut the courgettes into very thin slices - now cut the slices into quarters. Line a large, flat, non-stick pan with a thin layer of oil. Sauté the courgettes on a brisk heat until they become slightly brown. Lower the heat and cook for 10 to 12 minutes cover the pan with a lid (this helps the water to evaporate from the courgettes). Add parsley, garlic and a pinch of salt during the process.

2) Break the eggs into a mixing bowl and beat vigorously with a fork. Add milk, continue to beat. Add the grated cheese and continue to beat until you have a thickish liquid. Add a pinch of salt and pepper.

3) Remove the courgettes to a clean plate. Wipe your pan dry. Melt the butter in the pan on a low heat. Replace the courgettes into the pan. Pour the egg, milk and cheese mixture evenly into the pan and mix with the courgettes using a wooden spoon.

4) To make a quick, moist and juicy omelette, just raise the heat momentarily; avoid the mixture sticking. Allow the egg mixture to run underneath so that all the omelette is subject to the heat. Lower the heat - work the omelette with the spoon, bring the mixture to the centre of the pan, and your omelette should be ready for serving.

Preparation time: 10 minutes
Cooking time: 10 minutes

PANCAKES WITH SUGAR & LEMON (*)

2 PERSONS (THE SAME RECIPE IS USED FOR MORE PANCAKES, EXCEPT THAT THE QUANTITIES ARE INCREASED AS EXPLAINED BELOW)
50 G/2 OZ PLAIN FLOUR
1 EGG
2 TABLESPOONS SUGAR (WHITE)
1 DL/4 FL OZ MILK
2 TABLESPOONS BUTTER (FOR COOKING)
1/4 TEASPOON SALT
1/2 TABLESPOON OIL (SUNFLOWER)
1/2 LEMON JUICE

1) Sift the plain flour and put it into a clean mixing bowl. Add a pinch of salt. Beat the egg separately (whole) and pour into the centre of the flour (make a well in the flour). Add the oil, slowly pour in the milk, beating all the time until you get a nice batter (thickish liquid or paste).

2) Add 1 tablespoon butter into a non-stick shallow frying pan and melt the butter on a medium to high heat. Pour in just enough batter (slowly) to cover all the surface of the pan (for one pancake). Drop down the heat to medium to low, and cook until the underside is brown (2 to 4 minutes).

3) The experts will just flip the pancake over to the other side. I recommend, for the first time at least, sliding the pancake on to a plate, place another plate on top, reverse, and then slide the pancake back into the pan after adding another 1 tablespoon butter. When the underside is brown, slide on to a serving plate, add sugar and/or lemon juice, fold or roll up the pancake.

Now repeat the operation with your second pancake.

Note: More than two pancakes... if 4 pancakes, just double the flour and milk quantities: 8 pancakes... 200 g/7 oz flour, 4 dl/14 fl oz milk, but 2 eggs, salt becomes 1/2 teaspoon, step up the oil and butter in small measures, and increase sugar and lemon juice according to individual taste.

Preparation time: 5 minutes
Cooking time: 3 to 4 minutes
(XF = Extra-Fast)

SCRAMBLED EGGS (*)

2 PERSONS
4 FRESH EGGS
20 G/1 OZ BUTTER
2 TABLESPOONS MILK OR CREAM
PINCH OF SALT, AND BLACK PEPPER

1) Beat the eggs in a bowl or large glass adding two tablespoons of milk or cream, salt and pepper.

2) Melt the butter slowly in a shallow pan over a low to medium heat. Pour the egg mixture into the pan (when the butter has melted). Lower the heat when you pour in the egg mixture.

Allow the contents of the pan to slowly thicken remaining still light and a little fluid. Use a wooden spoon to bring the mixture into the centre of the pan.

If the mixture is too fluid/runny slightly increase the heat.

Remove and serve hot. Entire process should not take more than 3 to 4 minutes.

Note: You can also use just one tablespoon of milk or cream - depends on taste.

Preparation time: 15 minutes
Cooking time: 18 minutes

SCRAMBLED EGGS, MUSHROOMS, ONIONS & CHEESE (**)

2 PERSONS
80 G/3 1/2 OZ GRUYÈRE CHEESE, GRATED
90 G/4 OZ BUTTON MUSHROOMS (CHAMPIGNONS DE PARIS) FINELY CHOPPED
30 G/1 1/2 OZ SPRING ONIONS, FINELY CHOPPED (OPTIONAL)
PARSLEY, FINELY CHOPPED (3 TABLESPOONS WHEN CHOPPED)
1/4 GLASS WHITE WINE (USE REASONABLE QUALITY, NOT JUST CHEAP COOKING WINE)
4 FRESH EGGS
2 TABLESPOONS SINGLE CREAM
15 G/1/2 OZ BUTTER
3 TABLESPOONS OIL (SUNFLOWER)
SPRINKLE OF NUTMEG, SALT AND PEPPER
ABSORBENT KITCHEN PAPER

1) Prepare the mushrooms, spring onions and parsley (trim the mushroom stalks, peel and wash - retain the head of the spring onions and wash - wash the parsley and then remove the stalks and finely chop all three). Set aside.

2) Line a large, shallow, non-stick frying pan with oil, and heat. Place all the above ingredients (1) into the pan. Lightly fry in the oil on a medium heat for 10 minutes (the mushrooms and onions should be turning slightly brown).
Set aside on absorbent kitchen paper (to soak up the surplus oil). Wipe the inside of the pan dry with greaseproof or kitchen paper.

3) Crack open the eggs into a large bowl. Add the cream. salt pepper. Beat into a liquid using a fork.

4) Place the pan back over a medium heat, and melt a small pat of butter in the pan. Transfer the grated cheese to the pan. Add some nutmeg over the cheese as it melts. Pour in the white wine. Leave for a few minutes before adding the finely chopped mushrooms, onions and parsley (1).

5) Pour the egg mixture into the pan. Scramble and control the eggs and other ingredients (using a wooden spoon). If too liquid, slightly step up the heat. Avoid the mixture becoming too hot, or sticking to the pan.

Preparation time: 15 minutes
Cooking time: 45-55 minutes

EGGS A LA FLORENTINE (**)

4 PERSONS (AS A STARTER OR SECOND DISH - IF A MAIN DISH, WITH GOOD APPETITES, COUNT ONLY 2 PERSONS)
4 EGGS
500 G/1 LB 2 OZ SPINACH (FRESH OR FROZEN)
A LITTLE SALT AND PEPPER FOR THE SPINACH
BUTTER FOR GREASING THE BAKING TRAY
SMALL BUTTER FLAKES

<u>CHEESE SAUCE</u>
100 G/4 OZ PARMESAN CHEESE, GRATED
1.25 DL/5 FL OZ. SINGLE CREAM
1.25 DL/5 FL OZ. MILK
1 TEASPOON SALT, AND A LITTLE BLACK PEPPER
1 TEASPOON NUTMEG

1) First prepare the spinach - thaw if using frozen spinach by following the instructions on the wrapper. If you are using fresh spinach refer to page 72. Once the spinach is ready spread evenly in an overproof dish (which you have previously greased with a little butter).

2) <u>Preparing the sauce</u>
Use the bain-marie system (see under page 151) which, more time-consuming, is somewhat easier and will enable you to make a nice creamy cheese sauce.

Mix together the cream, milk. grated cheese, salt, pepper, and nutmeg in the saucepan (or other heat-proof vessel) which is standing or suspending in boiling water (keep the water just boiling). Continue to stir until you have a smooth, light, creamy sauce. When ready set aside to cool.

3) Make 4 wells or holes in the spinach (1). Crack open the eggs and pour (whole) one into each well.

4) Cover the spinach and eggs with the cheese sauce (2). Add a few butter flakes on top. Place the dish into a pre-heated oven (pre-heat for 10 minutes). Bake for 25 minutes at 180°C/350°F/Gas Mark 4. Serve hot.

EASY EXCELLENT COOKING GUIDE

PASTA, PASTA SAUCES AND PIZZAS

BRITISH AND EUROPEAN COOKING AT ITS BEST

Preparation time: 10-15 minutes
Cooking time: 35-40 minutes

MACARONI BELCAMPO (**)

Macaroni with a special savoury tomato sauce

2 PERSONS
200 G/7 OZ MACARONI   1 1/2 TO 2 LITRES/2 1/4 TO 3 1/2 PINTS WATER
1 1/2 TEASPOON SALT   1 TABLESPOON OIL [SUNFLOWER]

BELCAMPO SAUCE
70 G/3 OZ CONCENTRATED TOMATO PURÉE
1 TABLESPOON BASIL (FRESH), FINELY CHOPPED
1 TABLESPOON FRESH SAGE, FINELY CHOPPED
2 TABLESPOONS FRESH PARSLEY, MINCED
1/2 MEDIUM ONION, FINELY CHOPPED   2 CLOVES GARLIC, MINCED
1/2 BROTH CUBE   1 DL/4 FLOZ WHITE WINE
1 TEASPOON TARRAGON, FINELY CHOPPED (FRESH)   4 TO 5 TABLESPOONS OLIVE OIL
GRATED CHEESE   PEPPER AND SALT
5 TO 10 G/1/2 OZ BUTTER [IN RESERVE]

1) Cook the macaroni in 1 1/2 to 2 litres/2 1/4 to 3 1/2 pints salted water (first break the macaroni if the long variety). Place the macaroni into the water as soon as it boils, and keep the water boiling during 11 to 15 minutes cooking time. Check the cooking time on the wrapper. The macaroni when cooked should be "al dente" meaning just right, not under or overcooked. Do not cover with a lid during the cooking.
See the special section on cooking pasta (page 167)

2) Belcampo Sauce
Commence by preparing the basil, sage, parsley, onion, garlic and mix all together. Thinly cover the bottom of a large saucepan with olive oil, and heat. When the oil is hot put all the ingredients for the sauce into the pan, stir and brown. Empty the tomato purée into a clean glass, add 1 dl/4 fl oz white wine, stir well, pour this also into the pan. Be ready with 1/2 glass water in case too dry. Leave on a low heat for 15 to 20 minutes, adding 1/2 broth cube (crush the cube with a wooden spoon into the liquid). Add pepper and the tarragon. The sauce should not be too liquid. If it becomes too dry, add the butter held in reserve. Use a lid on the saucepan, and occasionally stir all the ingredients.

3) When the macaroni are cooked, drain off the water and transfer the macaroni into the saucepan and mix well with the sauce (which in the meantime is kept hot over a residual heat). Serve hot, with grated cheese according to taste.

Preparation time: 20-25 minutes
Cooking time: 55-60 minutes

MACARONI AU GRATIN (**)

2 TO 3 PERSONS
200 G/7 OZ MACARONI
1 TABLESPOON OIL (SUNFLOWER)
1 1/2 - 2 LITRES/2 1/2 - 3 1/2 PINTS WATER
1 1/2 TEASPOON SALT

<u>SAUCE</u>
250 G/9 OZ TOMATOES   50 G/2 OZ LEAN SMOKED BACON, CHOPPED
2 TABLESPOON TOMATO PUREE   2 CLOVES GARLIC, FINELY CHOPPED
1 LARGE ONION, FINELY CHOPPED
180 G/6 1/2 OZ MINCED MEAT (BEEF)
3 TABLESPOONS OIL (SUNFLOWER)
1 TEASPOON SALT   BLACK PEPPER
1 DL/4 FL OZ RED WINE
1 DL/4 FL OZ MEAT BROTH (OR 1/2 MEAT BROTH CUBE)
75 G/3 OZ GRATED CHEESE   FRESH BASIL, SAGE AND TARRAGON
A LITTLE BUTTER FOR GREASING THE OVENPROOF DISH.

Note: Should you wish to serve 4 persons, increase all the main ingredients by 25%

1) Start by washing and peeling the tomatoes - remove the stalks, cores and seeds (to remove the tomato skins first place the tomatoes into boiling water for 1 minute). Cut the tomatoes into small pieces. Peel both the onions and garlic and chop finely. Dice the bacon (cut into small cubes)

2) Cover the bottom of a large wide pan with a thin layer of oil. Heat the oil over a fairly sharp heat and sear the bacon.
Add the onions and garlic and brown slightly. Now add the minced meat and sear (takes the redness away) for 2 to 3 minutes. Add salt and pepper in the process.

3) Add the tomatoes as well as the tomato purée, basil, sage and tarragon. Continue to slowly stir - allow to cook for 5 minutes after which gradually pour in the red wine and meat broth but avoid making the sauce liquid. Reduce the heat slightly allow the contents to cook over a medium heat for 15 minutes at which time the thick sauce should be ready.

4) In the meantime, we shall cook the macaroni so that they are almost cooked when our sauce is ready. Break the macaroni once if they are the long variety. Bring the water to a boil, add salt, add the macaroni. Add a tbsp of oil (to prevent the pasta sticking). Stir occasionally, and do not cover the pan. Cooking time will be written on the wrapper, but under-cook by 2 minutes. Strain and pour cold water over the pasta and allow to dry.

5) Prepare an ovenproof dish by greasing it with a little butter (to avoid sticking). Add a first layer of macaroni, afterwards set down the layer of thickish meat sauce, and lastly a layer of macaroni over which you spread the grated cheese.

6) Pre-heat the oven for 10 minutes at maximum, and then allow the macaroni au gratin to bake for 20 minutes (in the centre of the oven) - 15 minutes at 200°C/400°F/Gas Mark 6, and 5 minutes at 180°C/350°/Gas Mark 4 (last 5 minutes is to have the macaroni crispy).

A variation consists of changing the sauce to a Béchamel sauce in which case refer to the preparation of Béchamel using 1 egg yolk, grated cheese and breadcrumbs on page 20. The Béchamel is poured over the macaroni [there are no layers] and the breadcrumbs are sprinkled over the top of the Béchamel sauce before placing it into the oven. Count from 15 to 20 minutes baking time in the oven.

Preparation time: 5-15 minutes
Cooking time: 15-25 minutes

MACARONI AL PESTO (*)

Macaroni with Pesto Sauce

2 PERSONS
200 G/7 OZ MACARONI
1 1/2 - 2 LITRES/2 1/2 - 3 1/2 PINTS WATER
1 1/2 TEASPOONS COOKING SALT
1 TABLESPOON OIL [SUNFLOWER]
GRATED CHEESE
PESTO SAUCE

1) Break the macaroni once if they are the long variety.
Bring the water to a boil, add salt, now add the macaroni. A tablespoon oil at this stage prevents the macaroni from sticking. Stir occasionally, and do not cover the saucepan.

2) For fresh macaroni count approx. 11 to 15 minutes cooking time; control for taste after 9 or 10 minutes.

3) Strain the macaroni when cooked and return them to the hot pan.
Mix in the Pesto sauce, stir well, and then serve hot.
Add grated cheese according to taste.

Note: For large types of pasta I usually leave just a little water in the pan to keep the pasta moist and hot, and I mix in 10 g butter prior to adding the Pesto.

For preparing your own Pesto Sauce refer to page 43.

Preparation time: 10 minutes
Cooking time: 20-25 minutes

PASTA WITH PEPPERS AND ANCHOVIES (**)

(It. Pasta ai Peperoni con Acciugata)

2 PERSONS
225 G/1/2 LB PASTA [ANY LARGE TYPE PASTA SUCH AS RIGATONI, PENNE, TORTIGLIONI, MACARONI, ETC.]
1 1/2 - 2 LITRES / 2 1/2 - 3 1/2 PINTS WATER
1 1/2 TEASPOON COOKING SALT
1 TABLESPOON OIL (SUNFLOWER)
2 TO 3 YELLOW PEPPERS
45 G/2 OZ ANCHOVIES (15 TO 18 FILLETS - LONG, FLAT IN OLIVE OIL)
3 GARLIC CLOVES, FINELY CHOPPED
4 TABLESPOONS OLIVE OIL
10 G /1/2 OZ BUTTER
GRATED CHEESE

1) Thoroughly wash the peppers and remove all the seeds and cores. Wash again, and reduce the peppers to small squares or strips (dice).

2) Bring the salted water to the boil. Add the pasta (one tbsp of oil prevents the pasta from sticking). Stir occasionally. Do not cover the saucepan with a lid. Cooking time is usually indicated on the wrapper of the pasta - for fresh pasta count 11 to 15 minutes, but taste after 9 or 10 minutes. When cooked, drain off the water, and return the pasta to the hot saucepan.

3) When the pasta is cooking prepare your anchovies and peppers. Take a clean pan, line with a thin layer of olive oil and heat. Do not overheat or fry the oil. Just let the oil remain hot. Crush the anchovies and garlic in the olive oil using a wooden spoon. Add the peppers, add 10 g butter. Control your heat. Cook for about 10 minutes on medium heat. Keep hot until your pasta is ready.

For serving, first serve the hot pasta on to the dishes, then add the sauce consisting of peppers and anchovies to each dish. Add grated cheese according to individual taste.

Note: See the special page on cooking pasta.

Preparation time: 15 minutes
Cooking time: 30-35 minutes

SPAGHETTI WITH BELCAMPO SAUCE (***)

2 PERSONS
200 G/ 1/2 LB SPAGHETTI
1 1/2 - 2 LITRES / 2 1/2 - 3 1/2 PINTS WATER
1 1/2 TEASPOONS COOKING SALT
1 TABLESPOON OIL (SUNFLOWER)
BELCAMPO SAUCE
75 G/3 OZ TOMATO PURÉE, CONCENTRATED
1 TABLESPOON FRESH BASIL, FINELY CHOPPED
1 TABLESPOON FRESH SAGE, FINELY CHOPPED
1 TABLESPOON FRESH PARSLEY, FINELY CHOPPED OR MINCED
1/2 MEDIUM ONION (30-40 G/ 1/2 OZ)
2 CLOVES GARLIC, MINCED
1/2 BROTH CUBE
1 DL/4 FL OZ WHITE WINE
1 TEASPOON TARRAGON
4-5 TABLESPOOONS OLIVE OIL
PEPPER AND SALT
5-10 G/ 1/2 OZ BUTTER (IN RESERVE)
GRATED CHEESE

See page 42 for preparing the Belcampo Sauce

1) Bring the salted water to a boil, add the spaghetti (for long spaghetti break into two). 1 tablespoon oil is added to prevent the spaghetti sticking.

2) Cooking time will depend on the quality, usually 11 minutes (refer to wrapper instructions). Do not cover with a lid. When the spaghetti are just right (al dente) remove and strain, add them to the sauce; mix thoroughly. Serve hot with grated cheese according to taste.

Note: See also "cooking pasta" in this book (page 167)

Preparation time: 5-10 minutes
Cooking time: 15-20 minutes

SPAGHETTI WITH PESTO SAUCE (*)

2 PERSONS
200 G/8 OZ SPAGHETTI
1 1/2 - 2 LITRES/2 1/2 - 3 1/2 PINTS WATER
1 1/2 TEASPOON COOKING SALT
1 TABLESPOON OIL (SUNFLOWER)
20 G/1 OZ BUTTER
3-4 TEASPOONS PESTO SAUCE (READY MADE, OR REFER TO PAGE 43 FOR THE PESTO SAUCE RECIPE)
100 G/4 OZ PARMESAN GRATED CHEESE

1) Salt the water, bring to a boil. Add the spaghetti (usually break into two if too long). Add 1 tablespoon oil (to prevent sticking). Cook until the spaghettis are "al dente" (time is usually indicated on the wrapper). Do not cover the saucepan, and make sure the water is always boiling.

2) When the spaghettis are cooked, strain, return the spaghettis to the hot saucepan, and serve immediately.

3) After serving, add a knob of butter and 1 1/2 teaspoons of Pesto sauce to each plate, stir well; now add the grated Parmesan according to individual taste - continute to mix well, and presto your spaghettis are now ready.

Note: See also "cooking pasta" on page 167.

Preparation time: 10 minutes
Cooking time: 15-20 minutes

TAGLIATELLE WITH TOMATOES, OLIVES, ANCHOVIES & BASIL (**)

2 OR 3 PERSONS
250 G/10 OZ TAGLIATELLE
400 /14 OZ RIPE TOMATOES
12 BLACK OLIVES, STONED (USE A DESEEDER, OR JUST HALVE THE OLIVES TO REMOVE THE STONES)
6 ANCHOVIES (FILLETS - LONG)
10 BASIL LEAVES (FRESH) FINELY CHOPPED
3 TABLESPOONS OLIVE OIL
3 CLOVES GARLIC, FINELY CHOPPED
30 G/1 1/2 OZ BUTTER
2 1/2 TEASPOONS SALT FOR 2 1/2 LITRES WATER
PEPPER

1) Peel the tomatoes. First boil the water, place the tomatoes into the boiling water (you will see that the tomatoes begin to burst). Remove the tomatoes, peel off the skins, and remove the seeds. Chop into small pieces. Set aside.

2) Pour 3 tbsp olive oil into a shallow saucepan. Bring to a low heat. Chop the garlic (or pass through a mincer). Add the garlic to the oil and crush the garlic into the oil with a wooden spoon. Similarly, mash the anchovies into the olive oil. Stir slowly, maintain a low heat, now place the tomatoes into the pan and continue to stir. Add black pepper, and 1/2 tsp salt. Leave the mixture to simmer for 10 to 15 minutes. Lastly, stir in the olives and basil just before removing the pan from the heat.

3) In the meantime, cook the tagliatelle in a large saucepan, filled with salted water (approx. 2 1/2 litres water and 2 tsp salt). Cooking time will depend on the quality. For fresh tagliatelle count 7 to 8 minutes. First boil the water, then add the tagliatelle, do not cover with a lid. Let the pasta boil all the time (without boiling over).

4) When the pasta is cooked "al dente" drain off the water, replace the pasta in the saucepan over a residual heat. Stir in the butter. Remove the pan, now stir in the sauce consisting of our tomatoes, garlic, anchovies, olives and basil. Stir well. Serve immediately. Use grated cheese according to individual taste.

Notes: Deseeding the tomatoes is not a "must" so do not let this worry you. Also, the quantity of water for pasta is a part of the golden rule, but if I just do not have such a large pan available I make do with less water. Adding a tbsp of olive oil to the water prior to boiling the tagliatelle avoids them sticking.

Preparation time: 15 minutes
Cooking time: 25-30 minutes

BELCAMPO SAUCE FOR PASTA (***)

2 TO 3 PERSONS
70 G/3 OZ CONCENTRATED TOMATO PURÉE
1 TABLESPOON FRESH BASIL, FINELY CHOPPED
1 TABLESPOON FRESH SAGE, FINELY CHOPPED
2 TABLESPOONS FRESH PARSLEY, MINCED
1/2 MEDIUM ONION (30 TO 40 G) FINELY CHOPPED
2 CLOVES GARLIC, MINCED
1/2 BROTH CUBE
1 DL/4 FL OZ WHITE WINE
1 TEASPOON TARRAGON (FRESH IF POSSIBLE) FINELY CHOPPED
4 TO 5 TABLESPOONS OLIVE OIL
PEPPER AND SALT
5 TO 10 G/ 1/2 OZ BUTTER (IN RESERVE)

1) Commence by preparing the basil, sage, parsley, onion, and garlic - mix all together.

2) Thinly cover the bottom of a large saucepan with olive oil, and bring to a medium heat, sufficient to brown, not too hot otherwise we shall burn the ingredients.
Place the ingredients (1) into the pan, stir and brown gently. Once browned, lower the heat immediately, and let your pan cool off - even remove the pan from the heat for a moment.

3) Empty the tomato purée into a clean glass, add 1 dl/4 fl oz white wine, mix well; pour this liquid into the pan which in the meantime you have placed back over a low heat.
Cook for 15 to 20 minutes on a low heat, rather very low than too high, but the mixture must still cook slowly.
Be ready with 1/2 glass water in case too dry.
Add 1/2 broth cube and crush with a wooden spoon into the liquid.
Add a pinch of pepper and the tarragon.
The mixture should not be too liquid, and not too solid. If it becomes too dry, add the butter which you have in reserve. Use a cover on the pan, and occasionally stir all the ingredients.

Note: You should time the cooking of the sauce to correspond with your pasta being ready.
It is very important to control the heat carefully; if the pan is too hot when you add the tomato mixture you risk spoiling the sauce.

Preparation time: 15-20 minutes

PESTO SAUCE (**)

3 TO 4 PERSONS
50 G/2 OZ FRESH BASIL (50 G AFTER STALKS REMOVE) FINELY CHOPPED
2 CLOVES GARLIC, FINELY CHOPPED
50 G/2 OZ PINE KERNELS
1 1/4 DL/JUST UNDER 1/4 PINT OLIVE OIL
25 G/1 OZ GRATED PECORINO OR PARMESAN CHEESE (4 TABLESPOONS)
1/4 TEASPOON SALT
PEPPER

1) Commence by lightly frying the pine kernels, just enough to colour them (1 to 2 minutes only) - make sure they do not burn. Allow to cool.

2) Grate your Pecorino cheese (if not available use Parmesan). Finely chop the garlic and basil.

3) Assemble the pine kernels together with the basil, garlic, salt and pepper, and put into a grinder (avoid making a thick paste). Better to use a mortar and pestle for grinding (if you are lucky enough to possess one). Commence slowly adding the olive oil, and stir (oil quantity can be increased or reduced depending how you like your Pesto). Lastly, add the grated cheese, and continue to stir slowly.

Retain in the refrigerator until use.

Note: Much depends on the quality and freshness of the basil.

Preparation time: 15-20 minutes
Cooking time: 70 minutes

BOLOGNESE SAUCE (***)

3 TO 4 PERSONS IDEAL WITH TAGLIATELLE AND OTHER TYPES OF PASTA

250 G/9 OZ MINCED BEEF
35 G/1 1/2 OZ LEAN BACON, DICED
1/2 CARROT, FINELY CHOPPED
1 STICK OF CELERY, FINELY CHOPPED
1 SMALL ONION, FINELY CHOPPED
1 CLOVE GARLIC, FINELY CHOPPED
2 TABLESPOONS TOMATO PURÉE
1 1/2 DL/1/4 PINT RED WINE (BETTER QUALITY AND DRY, IF POSSIBLE)
1-2 DL/4-7 FL OZ MEAT BROTH (MEAT STOCK, OR USE BROTH MADE WITH A MEAT CUBE)
1 TABLESPOON PARSLEY, CHOPPED FINELY
3 TABLESPOONS OLIVE OIL
FRESH BASIL
FRESH ROSEMARY
DRY OREGANO (IF AVAILABLE)
SALT AND BLACK PEPPER

1) Line a wide, deep pan with olive oil and heat slowly. Start by slightly browning the chopped onion, then add the carrot and celery and slowly brown. Add the minced meat and sear (remove the redness). Now add the diced bacon, season with salt and pepper, and stir and mix.

2) Stir in the garlic and tomato purée. Reduce the heat (even remove from the hot plate for a second) and pour the red wine slowly into the pan, stir, add a little more salt and pepper. Slightly bring back the heat and allow the wine to evaporate. Slowly pour in the meat broth. Continue to stir. Add the chopped basil, rosemary and the oregano. The contents of the pan should now be cooking on a medium heat and continue for 1 or 2 minutes.

3) Now cover the pan with a lid, and leave for one hour on a very low heat (just above simmering) so that the contents are still slowly cooking

4) Ensure that your Bolognese is not too dry. During the hour you will need to watch carefully, adding more meat broth as required. In fact, the crucial point is about 5 to 10 minutes before the hour has expired. The final substance should certainly not be dry, nor liquid, but fatty and creamy (pithy). You will probably need at this stage to add more meat broth and a largish knob of butter, and stir slowly, raising the heat for a minute, or two, and subsequently lowering the heat. The hot Bolognese is poured over the Pasta (in the warm pan) and mixed thoroughly. Add in the finely chopped parsley during the mixing). Bolognese sauce can also be pre-prepared and heated when ready for serving. This recipe is for 250 g/10 oz tagliatelle, as an example, for 2 to 3 (with excellent appetites) or 4 persons. Cooking tagliatelle see page 41.

A tip to liven-up Pasta with Bolognese Sauce - If on the next day your Pasta Bolognese is too dry add 3 tbsp olive oil, 1 glass red wine, celery salt, dry garlic and onion powder, 1 knob of butter, stir and mix - now cover and set the pan over a low heat for some 20/30 minutes

Preparation time: 25-30 minutes
Cooking time: 45 minutes

PIZZA (**)

2 PERSONS (LARGE PORTIONS FOR 2 - WILL SERVE 3 OR 4 IF A SECOND DISH OR STARTER)
450 G/1 LB PIZZA (BREAD) DOUGH "PÂTE À PAIN"
400 G/14 OZ FONTALE, OR FONTINA CHEESE - IF NOT AVAILABLE USE MOZZARELLA
1 LARGE TOMATO, OR TWO MEDIUM, THINLY SLICED
3 TO 4 SLICE BACON (WITHOUT FAT) CUT INTO SMALL SQUARES
1 SMALL TIN ANCHOVIES (6 TO 10 FILLETS)
1 DOZ. BLACK OLIVES, STONED
FRESH BASIL LEAVES, FINELY CHOPPED
GOOD SPRINKLE OF OREGANO

1) Use a round flan tin, diameter approx. 30 cm. Grease the tin well with a little butter (avoids dough sticking to the tin).
Roll out your dough so as to completely cover the tin including the sides of the tin. Use any surplus dough to make cross-sections and decoration. (Put down flour on a board when rolling the dough to avoid sticking).
Obviously prerolled dough is a time-saver if you have it available.

2) Make lots of holes in the dough once it is sitting in the tin (to avoid the dough rising)
Prepare the cheese by cutting it into small strips (thickness approx. 0.7/1 cm). Space the cheese to cover the entire inside of the tin. Now thinly slice the tomatoes and add them on top of the cheese. Now add the bacon (cut into small squares). Add the small anchovy fillets (separate from the bacon). Decorate the top of your pizza with the olives. Sprinkle the basil and oregano over the top of the pizza before placing it into the oven.
Fill any gaps in the pizza with remaining ingredients.

3) Preheat the oven for 10 minutes at 200°C/400°F/Gas Mark 6. Cook in the oven for 25 to 35 minutes at 180°C/350°F/Gas Mark 4. Control heat to avoid the pizza becoming too dry or burnt, and yet not underdone; pastry should become brown, or light-brown.

Preparation time: 20 minutes
Cooking time: 55 minutes

TO-MO-PIZZA (**)

2 TO 4 OR 6 PERSONS (GREAT APPETITES 2, SMALL APPETITES 4, OR AS A STARTER = 6 PERSONS)
450 G/1 LB PASTRY - IF POSSIBLE USE BREAD DOUGH ("PÂTE À PAIN") OTHERWISE USE PLAIN SHORTCRUST ("PÂTE À GATEAU")
900 G/2 LBS TOMATOES
150 G/5 OZ MOZZARELLA CHEESE   70 G/3 OZ BLACK OLIVES
FRESH BASIL   SALT & PEPPER
BUTTER (JUST ENOUGH FOR GREASING THE BAKING TIN)

1) First grease your ovenproof, shallow, flan tin or dish with a little butter (to avoid the contents sticking). Diameter of the tin should be approximately 26 cm/11" or slightly larger.
   Roll out your pastry to fit the tin including the sides of the tin (put flour down on your working surface before rolling out the pastry). Prick the pastry over the entire surface with a fork.

2) Pre-heat the oven for 10 minutes. Place your baking tin or dish into the oven (use a lower level in the oven).
   At this stage you are baking the pastry without any filling (your tin is empty except for the pastry).
   To avoid the pastry rising in the oven you need to cover the flat surface of the pastry with dried peas or rice (but first set down greaseproof paper to cover the pastry). Bake the pastry in the oven for 20 to 25 minutes, at 180°C 350°F/Gas Mark 4.

3) In the meantime, remove the skins, core and deseed the tomatoes. Cut into small pieces (for removing the skins, plunge the tomatoes into boiling water and leave for 1 or 2 minutes).
   Place the small tomato pieces into a saucepan. Boil the tomatoes on a low heat for a maximum of 15 to 20 minutes, sufficient time to evaporate any liquid in the tomatoes (time will depend on the quality of the tomatoes). Season with salt and pepper.
   Allow the tomatoes to cool and then spread them over the entire surface of the pastry (which you have removed in the meantime from the oven).

4) Cut the mozzarella into thin strips (size 1/2 cm/1/4"). Place the strips on top of the tomato surface making a lattice shape design. Now continue to decorate with the black olives. Lastly, sprinkle the basil over the entire contents. Bake in the oven (middle level) for 20 minutes at 180°C/350°/Gas Mark 4 until the pastry becomes a golden brown and the mozzarella melts.

Ideally served with a nice green salad.

EASY EXCELLENT COOKING GUIDE

RICE DISHES AND POLENTA

British and European Cooking at its Best

Preparation time: 15 minutes
Cooking time: 25 minutes

GREEN RICE (**)

2 PERSONS
200 G/7 OZ RICE (ROUND GRAIN)
PARSLEY, MINCED (8 TABLESPOONS PARSLEY BEFORE MINCING)
2 CLOVES GARLIC, MINCED
FRESH THYME
1 1/2 BROTH CUBES
PEPPER
7 1/2 DL/1 1/4 PINTS WATER - ADD AN EXTRA 2-4 DL/7-14 FL OZ DURING THE COOKING PROCESS
GRATED CHEESE
SALT

1) Wash the parsley. Remove stalks. Mince the parsley together with the cloves of garlic. Use a mincer. (before mincing, the parsley should equal 1/2 bunch or approx. 8 tablespoons). If mincing not possible just chop very finely.

2) Bring the water to a boil. Add the broth cubes and let them dissolve. Add the thyme and pepper.

3) Pour in the rice and cook over a medium heat for 20 to 25 minutes. Do not cover the saucepan with a lid. Check for taste after 20 minutes have elapsed - add a little salt as necessary.

4) 10 minutes prior to the rice being ready for serving, add the minced parsley and garlic, and continue to stir well so that it is absorbed by the rice. Result should be a thick green-coloured rice with broth.

Serve hot with grated cheese.

Note: When cooking rice ensure that the broth always just covers the top of the rice; as the rice expands add extra water so that the rice does not become dry.

Preparation time: 15 minutes
Cooking time: 35-50 minutes

RICE WITH ASPARAGUS (***)

2 PERSONS
450 G/1 LB ASPARAGUS
200 G/7 OZ RICE (ITALIAN-TYPE ROUND GRAIN)
10 G/1/2 OZ BUTTER
1 TABLESPOON PLAIN FLOUR
1 1/2 BROTH (CHICKEN) CUBES
1/2 BUNCH PARSLEY (2-3 TABLESPOON FINELY CHOPPED)
GRATED CHEESE
SALT

1) First wash the asparagus well. Cut off about 2 cm (hard ends) and throw away. Peel and trim the lower hard sides
Cook the asparagus in 1 litre/1 3/4 pints water (use a wide saucepan - depending on the length of the asparagus slice off the lower ends so that all the asparagus stems fit into your pan). Cooking time about 15 minutes (count 20 to 30 minutes for cavaillons asparagus - these are light in colour). Retain the asparagus water.

2) When cooked transfer the asparagus to a clean saucepan, over a residual heat, and serve them later as a second dish.

3) Mix the flour with the butter. Place in a clean pan over a low heat, stir. Pour your asparagus water into this saucepan (with the flour and butter). Add the broth cubes, bring to a boil. Stir well. Add the rice and cook for 20 minutes - stir occasionally.
Always ensure that the broth just covers the top of the rice. Add more of the asparagus water as necessary. Continue to stir.

4) Add the chopped parsley 2 to 3 minutes prior to serving. Stir well. Serve hot. Add grated cheese according to individual taste.

Note: The asparagus are dressed according to your own taste and served later as a second dish.

Preparation time: 15 minutes
Cooking time: 30 minutes

RICE JARDINIÈRE (**)

2 PERSONS
200 G/7 OZ RICE (ITALIAN-TYPE)
1 TIN MIXED CARROTS AND PEAS (450 G/1 LB)
20 G/1 OZ BUTTER
1 TABLESPOON WORCESTER SAUCE
GARLIC
ONION
CELERY SALT } DRY IN POWDER FORM
ROSEMARY
1/2 LITRE/1 PINT WATER (TO WHICH ADD 3 TO 4 DL/ 1/4 PINT TO 14 FL OZ)
1 TEASPOON SALT
GRATED CHEESE

1) Cook the rice in salted water for 20 minutes. Make sure the quantity of water is sufficient (as the rice boils and cooks continue to add water so that the rice is always just covered with water).
When the rice is cooked strain and return immediately to the hot saucepan adding 20g/1oz butter. See that the butter melts quickly and stir the rice in the process.

2) In the meantime prepare the peas and carrots. The easy quick solution which I like is a tin of precooked peas and carrots (you need only to heat). Drain off the liquid. Add the ingredients (Worcester sauce, garlic and onion, celery salt, rosemary) and mix well into the vegetables.

3) Now mix the peas and carrots with the rice. Mix extremely well before serving hot. Serve grated cheese.

Note: The key to success is to have the peas and carrots (or whatever vegetable you use) ready as soon as the rice is cooked so that both are hot when you mix before serving.

Preparation time: 15 minutes
Cooking time: 20 minutes

RICE SALAD (**)

2 PERSONS
200 G/7 OZ RICE (LONG GRAIN SUCH AS CAROLINE, OR UNCLE BEN)
1/2 LITRE/1 PINT WATER (ADD A FURTHER 2-3 DL/7 FL OZ - 1/2 PINT)
1/2 TEASPOON SALT
3 TABLESPOONS OLIVE OIL
PARSLEY, CHOPPED (2-3 TABLESPOONS)
1 DOZ. BLACK OLIVES, STONED
1/2 DOZ. ANCHOVIES [FILLETS CUT INTO HALVES]
1/2 DOZ. SARDINES IN OIL (CUT INTO HALVES)
1 TABLESPOON PESTO SAUCE
1 EGG, HARD-BOILED, SLICED
1 TOMATO CUT INTO SLICES, OR 6 CHERRY TOMATOES CUT INTO HALVES
2 DOZ. PRAWNS "CREVETTES" (COOKED, PEELED)

1) Cook the rice in salted water for 20 minutes. Ensure that the quantity of water is sufficient (as rice boils and cooks add more water so that the water always just covers the rice).
Check for taste, and when the rice is cooked strain it. Cool the rice completely by pouring cold water over the rice.

2) When the rice is cooled transfer it to a large salad bowl. Add 3 tablespoons olive oil and mix well.

3) Prepare all the various ingredients listed (parsley, olives, anchovies, sardines, egg, tomatoes, prawns and Pesto sauce) and mix with the rice thoroughly before serving. Even place in the refrigerator until serving.

Preparation time: 15 minutes
Cooking time: 30-35 minutes

RISOTTO (MILANESE) (***)

2 PERSONS
225 G/ 1/2 LB RICE [ITALIAN TYPE] FOR 3 PERSONS TAKE 250-300 G/9 - 11 OZ RICE
5 TABLESPOONS OIL [SUNFLOWER]
1 MEDIUM ONION, FINELY CHOPPED [APPROX. 40G/2 OZ]
1/2 GLASS WHITE WINE
1/2 GLASS MARSALA
PINCH OF SAFFRON (GOOD PINCH)
7.5 DL - 1 LITRE/1 1/2 - 1 3/4 PINTS STOCK, OR USE 2 CHICKEN BROTH CUBES
GRATED CHEESE, PARMESAN

1) Bring your water to the boil add the 2 broth cubes (use chicken or meat stock if available). Allow to simmer whilst you are preparing your rice.

2) Line the bottom of a large pan with oil, heat, add the chopped onion. Gently fry the onion so that the very small onion pieces turn brown. At this stage we add all the rice, and stir well so that the onion and oil mix with the rice.

3) Now slowly pour about half of your broth (see 1 above) over the rice until the rice is covered. Cook for 20 to 25 minute on a medium heat. Stir occasionally.

4) Important - as the rice is cooking it absorbs the liquid so we slowly pour in more broth. The rice should always be just covered by the broth. When the rice is cooked (check by tasting) you will have poured all the broth and the rice will appear thickish, floating in broth. Now remove from the heat.

5) Separately, mix the Marsala together with the white wine, adding also the saffron (my wife uses lots of saffron). Pour this liquid over the rice and stir slowly (the rice has to absorb all the wine, Marsala and saffron). Place over a low heat to keep warm.
Serve hot (with the broth) and add grated cheese to each plate, according to taste.

Note: This same recipe, in a classical cookery book, would probably read along the following lines: "prepare your stock. Brown the onion in oil, marry it with the rice, pour the stock over the rice so that the broth just covers it. Cook for 20 to 25 minutes, gradually adding the remainder of the stock. When cooked, add the white wine, Marsala, saffron, mix well. Serve with grated cheese".

Preparation time: 10-15 minutes
Cooking time: 25 minutes

RIZ GITANE (**)
Rice with Tomatoes and Bacon

2 TO 3 PERSONS (GENEROUS HELPINGS FOR 2)
200 G/7 OZ RICE (ITALIAN TYPE RICE)
250 G/1/2 LB TOMATOES
100 G/4 OZ LEAN, SMOKED BACON, DICED
1 MEDIUM SIZE ONION, FINELY CHOPPED
1 CLOVE GARLIC, FINELY CHOPPED
4 TABLESPOONS OIL (SUNFLOWER)
1 TABLESPOON TOMATO PURÉE
OREGANO (DRIED) OR BOUQUET GARNI
PARMESAN CHEESE, GRATED
2 MEAT (BEEF) BROTH CUBES
SALT AND PEPPER
1 LITRE/1 3/4 PINTS WATER

1) Wash the tomatoes and place them into water for 1 to 2 minutes (this will enable you to easily peel off the skins). Remove the skins and the cores. Chop the tomatoes into small pieces. Put aside.

2) Desolve broth cubes in boiling water, and allow to simmer until you are ready for stage (4).

3) Heat the oil in a deep, non-stick pan. Just brown the finely chopped onion and garlic. Now put in the chopped tomatoes (1). Mix and stir over a medium heat. Add the diced bacon. Continue to mix and stir. Leave for 5 minutes, still on a medium heat. Add a little salt and pepper. Add all the rice. Ensure that the rice is thoroughly mixed with all the other ingredients (onions, garlic, tomatoes, bacon, salt and pepper).

4) Pour in a quantity of broth (2) so that the broth just covers the rice. Cook the rice for 20 minutes (check cooking time on the wrapper). The broth should be bubbling (indicating the rice is cooking) over a medium heat - do not cover with a lid. Continue to keep the broth level just above the rice (by pouring in more broth). Stir occasionally.
Check the rice for taste after normal cooking time (at this stage you will have used all your broth).

5) Remove from the heat. Now thoroughly stir and mix in the tomato purée and oregano. Replace the pan over a low heat just to keep hot until serving. Serve with lots of grated cheese (according to taste).

Preparation time: 10 minutes
Cooking time: 15-25 minutes

POLENTA WITH CHEESE (**)

2 TO 4 PERSONS
250 G/9 OZ CORN-MEAL (MEAL OF MAIZE) (FR. SEMOULE DE MAÏS)
1 LITRE/1 3/4 PINTS FRESH MILK
20 G/1 OZ BUTTER
1/2 TEASPOON SALT
PORTIONS OF BLUE CHEESE SUCH AS GORGONZOLA, ROQUEFORT, AUVERGNE, OR DANISH BLUE

1) Heat the milk in a large, heavy-based saucepan, until just boiling.

2) Remove the saucepan and slowly add all the corn-meal with a little cooking salt; replace the saucepan back over a medium heat. Commence stirring immediately. Now reduce the heat (avoid lumps forming).

3) The corn-meal should cook over a low heat until it solidifies. Continue to stir throughout the cooking process. Cooking time can be between 5 and 15 even 20 minutes (check cooking time on the wrapper).
Just before the Polenta is ready for serving add a large knob of butter and mix well into the hot Polenta.

You serve yourself to the cheese according to individual taste, mixing the cheese with the Polenta, or simply eating the cheese alongside with the Polenta.

EASY EXCELLENT COOKING GUIDE

SALADS

BRITISH AND EUROPEAN COOKING AT ITS BEST

Preparation time: 15-20 minutes
Cooking time: 25-40 minutes

ASPARAGUS & BROCCOLI SALAD (*)

2 PERSONS
300 G/11 OZ ASPARAGUS
300 G/11 OZ BROCCOLI
2 X 1 TEASPOON SALT
VINAIGRETTE DRESSING (SEE VINAIGRETTE RECIPE ON PAGE 59)

1) Wash, peel the asparagus and remove the woody-type base on each asparagus. Cut each asparagus into 4 more or less equal parts, and place into boiling water in which 1 teaspoon of salt has been previously added.

2) Boil for 15 minutes (note - cooking time will vary with the quality of the asparagus; for example, white asparagus can take 30 minutes).

3) Proceed in the same manner with the broccoli, i.e. wash, trim into small florets and remove the stalks - the smaller stalks can be trimmed and cooked slightly ahead of the florets as they take longer. Cooking time for the broccoli is 15 minutes.

4) Both the asparagus and broccoli should be allowed to cool before placing into a salad bowl in which a vinaigrette dressing has been first added. Then toss the contents well before serving.

Note: Vegetable fans will often use the same water for different vegetables, although cooked separately. Instead of a glass of wine why not a glass of vegetable juice (i.e. the water in which you have cooked the vegetables).

Preparation time: 10-15 minutes

AVOCADO WITH PARMA HAM (*)

2 PERSONS
1 AVOCADO (NICE AND RIPE)
4 SLICES PARMA HAM (50 G/2 OZ)
DRESSING
2 TABLESPOONS OLIVE OIL
1 TEASPOON LEMON JUICE
1/2 CLOVE GARLIC, FINELY CHOPPED
2 TO 3 TEASPOONS PARSLEY, CHOPPED VERY FINE
SALT AND BLACK PEPPER

1) Peel off the avocado's outer skin, cut in half and remove the stone. Cut each half of the avocado into four slices. Wrap the ham around the avocado slices (each slice of Parma ham will contain two pieces of avocado).

2) Prepare the dressing in a mixing bowl, or glass, and mix well. Pour the dressing over the individual portions only when serving.

Preparation time: 15-25 minutes

CAPRICCIOSA SALAD (*)
("Whimsical" Salad)

> 2 TO 6 OR MORE PERSONS (SELECT QUANTITIES ACCORDING TO NUMBER OF PERSONS)
> THIS IS A MAIN DISH FOR 2 PERSONS
> 1 RED PEPPER (1/4 TO 1/2 OF A PEPPER FOR 2 PERSONS)
> 1 GREEN PEPPER ("   "   "   ")
> 1 YELLOW PEPPER ("   "   "   ")
> 1 SMALL CUCUMBER (12 THIN SLICES FOR 2 PERSONS) BLACK & GREEN OLIVES (10 OF EACH FOR 2 PERSONS) GRATED CARROTS (1/2 CARROT FOR 2 PERSONS) SMALL CHERRY TOMATOES (8 TO 10 FOR 2 PERSONS)
> TREVISAN (TREVISAN IS AN ITALIAN SALAD VEGETABLE WITH LARGE RED LEAVES - NOT ALWAYS EASY TO FIND; IF NOT AVAILABLE SELECT A SALAD OF YOUR CHOICE)
> OLIVE OIL (5 TABLESPOONS FOR 2 PERSONS)
> VINEGAR (1 TO 2 TEASPOONS FOR 2 PERSONS)
> SALT AND BLACK PEPPER

This is a salad for 2,4,6 or more persons. If only 2 persons you will need at the most a half of each pepper, which means you will have three halves remaining (see recipe on page 81 on how to use the remainder of the peppers). Similarly, the cucumber, black and green olives, tomatoes, carrots and salad have to be measured according to the quantities required (indications above are only for 2 persons).

1) Wash the peppers, cut into large slices, remove cores and seeds, wash again. Now cut into very thin strips, length fairly short. Wash the cucumber and tomatoes, and slice the cucumber, and halve the small cherry tomatoes. Grate the carrot after washing and peeling.

2) Make sure that you have carefully washed your salad vegetable (Trevisan or another with large leaves) after which set aside the quantity required, and cut into medium size leaves.

3) First place your salad leaves into the salad bowl, then add and decorate with all the other ingredients. I have yet to see a more decorative salad bowl !

4) Mix your oil and vinegar, salt and pepper, and add to the salad bowl just before serving, and remember to toss extremely well.

Note: For oil, vinegar, salt and pepper, step up the quantities in small measures for more than two persons.

Preparation time: 20 minutes
Cooking time: 30-35 minutes

COURGETTES & CAULIFLOWER SALAD (*)

4 PERSONS   (AS A STARTER OR EVEN AS A MAIN DISH)
450 G/1 LB COURGETTES
900 G/2 LBS CAULIFLOWER
2 TEASPOONS COOKING SALT
DRESSING
6 TABLESPOON OLIVE OIL
1 TABLESPOON VINEGAR
1/2 TEASPOON MUSTARD
WORCESTER SAUCES (JUST A SPRINKLE)
SALT AND PEPPER

1) First wash the courgettes. Trim off the ends. Cook for 8 minutes (until tender) in boiling salted water (cover the pan with a lid). Water should be boiling all the time.
When cooked, strain but retain the cooking water. Allow the courgettes to cool. Now slice or dice fairly fine.

2) Trim the cauliflower into florettes (cut away outer leaves and stalks, etc.) wash, cook in boiling salted water for 20 to 25 minutes, until tender. Use the same water as for the courgettes.
Sprinkle a little vinegar into the water to avoid the cauliflower smell.
Keep a lid on the pan (water should be boiling all the time).
When cooked, strain and allow to cool.

3) Prepare your salad dressing - mix well in a very large salad bowl. Now add the courgettes and cauliflower (all finely sliced). Toss extremely well before serving.

Preparation time: 15 minutes
Cooking time: 20-25 minutes

FENNEL SALAD (*)

2 PERSONS
450 G/1 LB FENNELS
1 SMALL, OR 2 VERY SMALL ONIONS, FINELY CHOPPED
1 CLOVE GARLIC, FINELY CHOPPED
3 ANCHOVY FILLETS, SLICED INTO 2 OR 3 PARTS
2 BACON RASHERS, DICED (CUT INTO SMALL SQUARES)
2 MEDIUM TOMATOES, SLICED
1 TEASPOON LEMON JUICE
1 TEASPOOON SALT

SAUCE
4 TABLESPOONS OLIVE OIL
1 TEASPOON VINEGAR
1/4 TEASPOON MUSTARD
1 TEASPOON WORCESTER SAUCE
1/2 TEASPOON SALT
BLACK PEPPER

1) Wash the fennels, cut away all stalks, sprigs, and any tough outer leaves, leaving just the bulbs. Cut the bulbs into four parts, wash again thoroughly. Boil in salted water for 20/25 minutes. Cover with a lid. Add 1 teaspoon lemon juice to the water.

2) Prepare the salad sauce as described above - mix all the ingredients well.

3) Strain the fennels when they are cooked, allow to cool, chop or cut into small pieces. Now pour the salad sauce over the fennels and toss well.

4) In the meantime, prepare the other ingredients (onions, garlic, anchovies, bacon, tomatoes) and when ready for serving add these ingredients to the fennels. At this stage I add another tablespoon of olive oil and toss extremely well before serving.

This makes an excellent salad.

Preparation time: 15-20 minutes
Cooking time: 30-35 minutes

FRENCH BEANS IN SALAD (*)

2 PERSONS
400 G/14 OZ FRENCH GREEN BEANS
2 SMALL ONIONS, FINELY CHOPPED
PARSLEY, CHOPPED (2-3 TABLESPOONS WHEN CHOPPED)
1/2 TEASPOON MUSTARD
1/2 LEMON JUICE
1 TABLESPOON VINEGAR
5 TABLESPOONS OLIVE OIL
1 LARGE TOMATO SLICED, OR 6 VERY SMALL TOMATOES CUT INTO HALVES
PEPPER
SALT

1) Trim and taper the green beans (remove tops and tails) and cut into halves, wash.

2) Cook in salted boiling water for 30-35 minutes (not too much water). Cooking time depends on thickness of the beans. When cooked, strain.

3) When cool and dry place the beans in a serving bowl (a rapid way of cooling is to pour cold water over the beans, but make sure they are completely dry before adding the dressing - what you do not need is water mixing with your salad dressing).
Add the chopped onions, parsley and tomatoes.

4) Prepare your dressing on the side. Start with the olive oil, vinegar, lemon juice, mustard, salt and pepper. Mix well, and pour this dressing over the beans. Toss extremely well before serving.

Preparation time: 15 minutes
Cooking time: 10 minutes

GREEN SALAD WITH DRESSING (*)

2 OR 3 PERSONS
1 LETTUCE, OR EQUIVALENT SUCH AS MÂCHE, DANDELION, FRISÉE ("RAMPON, SALADINE, BATTAVIA")
5 TABLESPOONS OLIVE OIL
1 TEASPOON VINEGAR ("VINAIGRE DE VIN ROUGE")
1 TEASPOON WORCESTER SAUCE
1/2 TEASPOON MUSTARD (FRENCH)
1 SMALL ONION, FINELY CHOPPED
2 EGGS, HARD-BOILED, SLICED
1 TIN OF TUNA (50 G/2 OZ) STRAINED AND CUT INTO SMALL SLICES
1 MEDIUM TOMATO, SLICED
SALT
PEPPER

1) Thoroughly wash the lettuce (or other green vegetable which you are using). Shake dry. Wash the tomato before slicing.

2) Use a large salad bowl. Pour in the olive oil, vinegar, Worcester sauce, add mustard, pepper and salt, mix well.

3) Now add the green salad (cut into small leaves). Add the chopped onion, tuna fish pieces, tomato slices and hard-boiled eggs (sliced).
Just before serving thoroughly mix and toss all the contents of your salad bowl, and your salad is ready.

Note: Eggs take 10 minutes to hard-boil - plunge into cold water - when cool, tap and peel the shells before slicing.

Preparation time: 15-20 minutes
Cooking time: 5 minutes

ITALO-LYONNAISE SALAD (*)

2 PERSONS
1 LETTUCE, OR OTHER VEGETABLE SUITABLE FOR SALADS
2 SMALL TOMATOES, SLICED
1 SMALL ONION, FINELY CHOPPED
1 CLOVE GARLIC, FINELY CHOPPED
3 SLICES OF BACON, DICED [REMOVE FAT]
1 OR 2 SLICES OF TOAST BREAD, CUT INTO SMALL CROÛTONS
LEMON JUICE (1/2 LEMON)
1 TEASPOON WORCESTER SAUCE
4 TABLESPOONS OLIVE OIL
2 TABLESPOONS OIL (SUNFLOWER)
1 TABLESPOON PESTO SAUCE
PEPPER & SALT

1) Wash the lettuce thoroughly, and dry. Cut the lettuce into small leaves. Wash the tomatoes, cut them into small slices.

2) Pour the olive oil into a large salad bowl, add the Worcester sauce, lemon juice, salt and pepper, and mix. Add the lettuce leaves, tomato slices, chopped onion and garlic.

3) Line a shallow frying pan with oil, heat, and add the bacon squares and croûtons; fry until the croûtons become crisp and brown. Add the bacon and croûtons to the salad bowl, and mix.

4) Just prior to serving add the Pesto sauce; mix and toss extremely well.

Preparation time: 10-15 minutes
Cooking time: 25-30 minutes

KOHLRABI SALAD (*)

2 PERSONS
1 LARGE KOHLRABI, OR 2 MEDIUM SIZE KOHLRABI
10 G / 1/2 OZ BUTTER
1 TEASPOON & 1/2 TEASPOON SALT
BLACK PEPPER
2 TABLESPOONS OLIVE OIL
FRESH THYME

1) Wash, peel the kohlrabi, and slice into small pieces (cooks quicker).

2) Bring the salted water to a boil, add the kohlrabi slices not too much water. Cover the saucepan with a lid. Cook for 25 to 30 minutes until tender, strain.

3) Mash the kohlrabi with a fork, adding 10g / 1/2 oz butter. Now allow to cool. Add 1/2 teaspoon salt, black pepper, olive oil, a little fresh thyme, and mix well with the kohlrabi ready for serving.

Preparation time: 15-20 minutes
Cooking time: 25-30 minutes

LENTIL SALAD (*)

2 PERSONS
100 G/4 OZ (BROWN) LENTILS (ALREADY SOAKED)
4 SMALL TOMATOES, CUT INTO HALVES
PARSLEY, FINELY CHOPPED
1 EGG, HARD-BOILED, THINLY SLICED
2 SMALL ONIONS, FINELY CHOPPED
1 OR 1 1/2 TEASPOONS COOKING SALT FOR THE LENTILS
<u>SAUCE</u>
5 TABLESPOONS OLIVE OIL
1/2 TEASPOON VINEGAR
1/2 TEASPOON MUSTARD
PINCH OF BLACK PEPPER
1/2 TEASPOON SALT

1) Salt the water and bring to a boil. Add the lentils and cook for 30 to 40 minutes (wrapper will usually indicate exact cooking time).

2) When cooked, remove and strain. Allow to cool by pouring cold water over the lentils. Dry well before placing the lentils into a serving bowl. Decorate with the egg slices, tomatoes, onions, and parsley.

3) For the sauce, take a separate receptacle, pour in the olive oil, vinegar, mustard, salt, pepper, and mix very well.

Just before serving, pour the sauce over the lentils and toss extremely well.

Preparation time: 5-10 minutes
(XF = Extra-Fast)

MOZZARELLA AND TOMATO SALAD (*)

2 PERSONS
2 MEDIUM TOMATOES
150 G/5 OZ MOZZARELLA CHEESE
4 TABLESPOONS OLIVE OIL
FRESH BASIL LEAVES, CHOPPED
PEPPER AND SALT

1) First wash the tomatoes and then cut them into small thin slices; place them into a salad bowl.

2) Drain off any water from the Mozzarella. Slice the Mozzarella into small pieces and add to the salad bowl.

3) Mix the basil leaves with the tomatoes and Mozzarella. Pour the olive oil over the salad bowl contents and toss and mix well adding a little salt and pepper according to individual taste.

Preparation time: 20-30 minutes

SALADE NIÇOISE (**)

2 TO 4 PERSONS (A MAIN COURSE FOR 2 PERSONS, AND A FIRST COURSE FOR FOUR)

- 1 LARGE LETTUCE
- 3 SMALL TO MEDIUM TOMATOES, QUARTERED
- 1 CAN TUNA FISH. (100-150 G/4 - 5 OZ)
- 6 ANCHOVY FILLETS, LONG, SLICED INTO HALVES OR MORE
- 15 BLACK OLIVES. STONED
- 1 SMALL CAN OF FRENCH GREEN BEANS, PRE-COOKED
- 1 GREEN PEPPER, CORE AND SEEDS REMOVED
- 2 EGGS, HARD-BOILED, CUT INTO SLICES
- PARSLEY, FINELY CHOPPED (2 TO 3 SPRIGS)
- 1 TABLESPOON FRESH BASIL, FINELY CHOPPED
- 6 TABLESPOONS OLIVE OIL
- 1 TABLESPOON VINEGAR
- 1/2 TEASPOON SALT
- BLACK PEPPER
- 1 TEASPOON FRENCH MUSTARD

1) Have small plates available for the various ingredients. Wash the lettuce (dry well with a cloth). Wash the pepper and cut it into large slices, remove seeds and cores, wash again. Cut the pepper slices into thin small strips or dice. Wash the tomatoes and cut each into 4 parts (quartered). Hard boil the eggs (10 minutes) and slice with an egg cutter or knife. Remove the tuna fish. anchovies. and beans from their respective cans or tins, and drain off the liquids (liquids not needed). The olives should have stones removed.

2) <u>Salad Dressing</u>

Pour the olive oil into a large salad bowl (6 tbsp or more) add the vinegar, mustard, salt and pepper, and mix well (until the mustard is absorbed).

3) <u>Presenting the "Salade Niçoise"</u>

Place the larger lettuce-leaves around the bottom of the salad bowl. Smaller leaves on top and at sides. Add the green beans, tuna fish, tomatoes and egg slices (if difficult to cut the tuna just place the pieces into the middle of the bowl). Finish by placing the anchovies, olives and the small pepper strips. Sprinkle the chopped parsley and basil over the top. Your "salade niçoise" is now ready for serving (after you have tossed the salad extremely well so that oil penetrates).

Preparation time: 20 minutes

SPINACH AND AVOCADO SALAD (*)

2 PERSONS
350 G/12 OZ SPINACH
1 MEDIUM ONION FINELY CHOPPED
2 EGGS, HARD-BOILED, SLICED
2 TABLESPOONS BUTTER
1 AVOCADO (RIPE)
1/4 TEASPOON SALT
PEPPER
<u>SAUCE</u>
1/2 GLASS VINAIGRETTE SAUCE

Note: I suggest using deep-frozen spinach (see wrapper for special instructions).

If you use fresh spinach refer to page 72.

1) Add sufficient water in the pan to just cover the spinach (frozen or partially defrozen). Use a medium heat to defreeze). Continue to heat for 10 to 12 minutes. Add a little salt to the water.
Strain and allow the spinach to cool. Squeeze out any water (otherwise it remains soggy).

2) Peel off the outer skin of the avocado, remove the stone, and chop the avocado into small pieces. Place in a separate bowl, add the egg slices.

3) Take a clean pan, place over a brisk heat, melt 2 tablespoons butter, add the chopped onion and brown. Pour the contents of the pan over the spinach. Toss the spinach. Now add the avocado and egg slices, a little pepper, and mix well.

4) <u>Vinaigrette</u>
On the side prepare your vinaigrette sauce (refer to page 73). Before serving, pour the vinaigrette over the salad and toss well. If too dry add more olive oil.

Preparation time: 10-15 minutes
Cooking time: 10 minutes
Standing time: 30 minutes

SPINACH SALAD (*)

2 PERSONS (SERVED AS A STARTER, OR JUST AS A SALAD).
700 G/1 1/2 LB FRESH SPINACH
1 OR 2 LEMONS
4 TABLESPOONS OLIVE OIL
SALT
PEPPER

1) Wash the spinach thoroughly (usually this means washing 3 to 4 times or more) Remove the stalks. Take a large saucepan, half fill with water, and cook the spinach for 9 to 10 minutes in salted water (or pressure-cook for 3 minutes).

2) When cooked, drain off the water, leave the spinach to cool for 30 minutes or more. Now squeeze the remaining water out of the spinach (best way is to squeeze the spinach between the hands).
Remember that spinach reduces in volume after cooking, so what looks like a large amount for 2 persons becomes hardly enough at the end.

After serving, run your knife through the spinach as if chopping, add olive oil, pepper and salt according to individual taste. Lastly, squeeze 1/2 lemon juice over the spinach on each plate, mix well with the oil and lemon juice, salt and pepper, and your spinach salad is ready.

Preparation time: 5 minutes

VINAIGRETTE SALAD DRESSING (*)

2 TO 4 PERSONS
3 TO 4 TABLESPOONS OLIVE OIL
1 TEASPOON VINEGAR (RED WINE VINEGAR)
1/4 TEASPOON MUSTARD (FRENCH)
SALT AND PEPPER TO TASTE

Mix the above ingredients before adding a green salad
Toss the salad before serving

Preparation time: 5-10 minutes

SPECIAL SALAD DRESSING (*)

2 TO 4 PERSONS
4 TO 5 TABLESPOONS OLIVE OIL
1 TABLESPOON SUNFLOWER OIL
1 TABLESPOON VINEGAR (RED WINE VINEGAR)
1/2 TABLESPOON LEMON JUICE
1/4 TEASPOON MUSTARD
1/4 TEASPOON SALT
PINCH OF PEPPER

Mix well before adding your green salad, and then toss and mix before serving.

Note: This last salad dressing is not very conventional - in fact, there is no end to the variety of salad dressings one can make. I particularly like this dressing.

Preparation time: 15-20 minutes
Standing time: 45 to 60 minutes

SPANISH SUMMER SALAD - PIPIRRANA (*)

4 TO 6 PERSONS
1 RED PEPPER
1 GREEN PEPPER
1 SMALL CUCUMBER
1 SMALL ONION, FINELY CHOPPED OR MINCED
2 TO 3 MEDIUM TOMATOES (350-450 G/3/4 - 1 LB DEPENDING WHETHER 4 OR 6 PERSONS)
3 TO 4 CLOVES GARLIC, CRUSHED/MINCED
3 TO 4 TABLESPOONS (RED WINE) VINEGAR
SALT AND BLACK PEPPER
5 TO 6 TABLESPOONS OLIVE OIL

1) Use a large salad bowl. Prepare the peppers as outlined on page 82. Peel the cucumber, remove seeds and wash. Dice all the peppers and cucumber. Place the peppers and cucumber into the salad bowl.

2) Remove the tomato skins (place the tomatoes into boiling water for 1 minute so as to easily remove the skins). Remove the hard cores and seeds, and then dice or mash. Add to the salad bowl.

3) The sauce: pour the olive oil into a clean bowl - add the vinegar, salt and pepper. Mince or crush the garlic, chop the onion very finely or mince, and add both to the sauce, mixing at the same time.
Now pour the sauce over the contents of your salad bowl, toss well, and allow to stand in the refrigerator for 45 minutes to 1 hour before serving.

This makes a delicious refreshing salad ideal in the hot summer months. Use your judgement with the vinegar and salt and pepper, whether or not you like your salad very spicy.

EASY EXCELLENT COOKING GUIDE

VEGETABLES

BRITISH AND EUROPEAN COOKING AT ITS BEST

Preparation time: 20 minutes
Cooking time: 1 hr. 10

ARTICHOKES "PROVENCALE" (**)

> 2 PERSONS (OR 4 PERSONS AS A STARTER)
> 8 VERY SMALL ARTICHOKES (WHEN IN SEASON)
> 100 G/4 OZ BACON, CHOPPED
> 70 G/3 OZ ONION, CHOPPED (1/2 A LARGE ONION)
> 3 X 2 TABLESPOONS OLIVE OIL
> 1/2 LEMON JUICE
> THYME, FRESH, & REMOVED FROM THE STALKS
> 2-3 DL/7 FL OZ-1/2 PINT WHITE WINE (GOOD QUALITY)
> SALT AND PEPPER

1) Cut off and dispose of the artichoke stems - wash the artichokes. Place each artichoke flat (horizontal) and using a sharp knife cut or chop off all the top ends of the leaves, with just the body of the artichoke remaining (this is easy with very tiny artichokes, but larger artichokes require the removal of the far thicker leaves in the cutting or chopping process).
With the body of the artichoke still flat (preferably on a chopping board) slice the artichoke lengthways into very small parts. Now remove the small "beard" known as the hairy choke (part of the inside of the artichoke - note that tiny artichokes have almost no "beard") Squeeze lemon juice over the artichokes.

2) Using a large, shallow pan, heat the oil, add the chopped onions, bacon and thyme Sprinkle a little salt and pepper over the top, and brown all these ingredients on a brisk heat. Remove from the pan and set aside.

3) Add more oil to the pan, heat, place in the small artichoke slices and brown. Now replace all the other ingredients (2) into the pan and mix well with the artichokes. Add 1 dl/ 4 fl oz of white wine - cover with a lid and cook on a moderate heat for 40 to 50 minutes. After 10 minutes add a little more salt and pepper, another 1 dl/4 fl oz of white wine, and stir well. Cover and allow the cooking process to continue.

If the pan is too dry, add a little water. I usually add more white wine and water, but this is a question of taste.

An interesting and tasty dish, but finding the very tiny artichokes is not easy.

Preparation time: 15-20 minutes
Cooking time: 55 minutes

CAULIFLOWER AU GRATIN (***)

2 TO 3 PERSONS
1 LARGE CAULIFLOWER (700 G/1 1/2 LBS)
3 TABLESPOONS PLAIN FLOUR   30 G/1 1/2 OZ BUTTER
3 DL/ 1/2 PINT MILK   1/2 TABLESPOON NUTMEG
1 EGG (YOLK-ONLY)   4 TO 5 TABLESPOONS OIL (SUNFLOWER)
50 G/2 OZ GRATED CHEESE
1 CLOVE GARLIC, PEELED & FINELY CHOPPED
1 VERY SMALL ONION, PEELED & FINELY CHOPPED
2 TABLESPOONS DRY BREADCRUMBS   1 TABLESPOON VINEGAR
BLACK PEPPER & COOKING SALT

1) Trim the cauliflower into florettes. Wash and cook in lightly salted boiling water. Sprinkle a little vinegar into the water (to avoid the smell). Cover your pan with a lid. When tender (after 15 minutes) strain. Do not let the cauliflower cook completely.

2) Line the bottom of a clean, shallow, frying pan with oil - heat, and brown the garlic, onion and cauliflower on a brisk heat. Sprinkle a little salt and pepper over the top. (Note - if there is too much cauliflower for the size of the pan, brown the contents in two or more steps).

3) Take a clean pan - melt the butter. Reduce the heat, add the flour slowly, stir on a low heat, pour in the milk. Continue to stir to obtain a thickish liquid (almost a cream, without lumps forming). Slowly step up the heat, add the salt, pepper and nutmeg. Remove from the heat. Continue to stir. Now place back over a low heat, add the egg yolk and grated cheese mixture (beat the yolk and grated cheese together beforehand). Keep on stirring until you produce a smooth creamy mixture.

4) Prepare an ovenproof dish (grease it with a little butter on the sides and bottom to avoid the contents sticking).
Cover the bottom of the dish with a first layer of the mixture (3). Add all the cauliflower on top; add a final top coat of the mixture (3). Lastly, sprinkly the breadcrumbs evenly over the top.

5) Place in a pre-heated oven, and cook for 20 minutes at 200°C/400°F/Gas Mark 6 until the topping is almost golden brown.

Note: The cauliflower is only about 1/2 or 3/4 cooked in (1) above; otherwise it would be overcooked by the time you reach the end in (5).

Preparation time: 15 minutes
Cooking time: 60 minutes

FENNELS AU GRATIN (***)

2 OR 3 PERSONS
4 MEDIUM FENNELS (600 G/1 1/4 LB)
4 TABLESPOONS OIL (SUNFLOWER)
2 1/2 DL/8 FL OZ MILK
2 TABLESPOONS PLAIN WHITE FLOUR
20 G/1 OZ BUTTER
1/2 DL/2 FL OZ WHITE WINE
1 EGG
3 TABLESPOONS GRATED CHEESE
2 TABLESPOONS BREADCRUMBS "PANURE BLONDE"
1/2 TABLESPOON NUTMEG
COOKING SALT
GARLIC (DRY - POWDER)
BLACK PEPPER

1) Wash the fennels, cut away all stalks, sprigs, and other tough leaves, with just the bulbs remaining. Cut the bulbs into small pieces, wash again. Now chop the fennels into smaller pieces (dice).

2) Line the bottom of a large frying pan with a thin layer of oil and bring to a high heat. Add the fennels, pepper, salt and garlic. Bring the fennels to a brown colour (takes a little time for water to come out of the fennels). Cover the pan to avoid splashing.

3) Add a little water, reduce the heat, and cook in the same pan for about 15 minutes. Add 1/2 dl white wine slowly. Mix the fennels well (fennels will still be a little hard and not completely cooked).

4) In the meantime you will have greased an ovenproof gratin dish with butter (to avoid sticking). Transfer the fennels into this dish.

5) Take a clean saucepan. Add flour, butter using a low heat, stir slowly. Add the milk gradually, continue to stir. Keep the heat low and not too hot. Continue mixing flour, butter and milk; add 1 egg (complete) stir. Add nutmeg, grated cheese, continue stirring. Result should be a thick creamy substance.

6) Spread the mixture evenly over the fennels (in the dish) Add a sprinkling of breadcrumbs,
Place the dish in a preheated oven (preheat for 10 minutes) and leave for 30 minutes at 180°C/350°F/Gas Mark 4.

Preparation time: 15 minutes
Cooking time: 30 minutes

FENNELS WITH WHITE WINE (**)
"Fenouils au Vin Blanc"

2 PERSONS
700 G/1 1/2 LB FENNELS
1 1/2 TO 2 1/2 DL/1/4 PINT TO 8 FL OZ WHITE WINE
3 TABLESPOONS OIL (SUNFLOWER)
1/2 CHICKEN BROTH CUBE
SALT AND ONE PINCH OF BLACK PEPPER

1) Wash the fennels, cut away all stalks, sprigs, and any tough outer leaves, leaving just the bulbs. Cut the bulbs into small parts, wash again thoroughly. Chop the fennel bulbs into very small pieces ready for frying (diced) and dry them (by pressing in a cloth).

2) Cover the bottom of a large frying pan with a thin layer of oil and heat. Now add the fennels, cover with a lid, and brown on a high heat for 7 to 8 minutes. Mix and turn occasionally, add salt, pepper and 1 dl/4 fl oz wine, plus 1/2 broth cube.

At this stage, fennels should be slowly turning brown. Turn to medium heat and cook for 15 to 20 minutes. Add the remainder of the wine slowly, and if the pan becomes too hot or dry correct with a little water and/or reduce the heat.

Preparation time: 15 minutes
Cooking time: 15-20 minutes

PEPPERS WITH ANCHOVIES (*)

2 PERSONS
2 PEPPERS, DICED
50 G/2 OZ CAN OF ANCHOVIES (IN OIL)
3 TO 4 TABLESPOONS OLIVE OIL
1 GARLIC CLOVE, MINCED OR CRUSHED
20 G/1 OZ BUTTER

1) Wash the peppers and cut into large parts so as to easily remove the cores and all the seeds. Wash again. Now dice the peppers (reduce to small squares or strips).

2) Put the anchovies (with any oil from the tin) and the garlic (minced) with a little olive oil into a non-stick frying pan - bring to a brisk heat for 2 minutes. Now add the diced peppers to the pan.

3) Lower heat, stir to avoid the anchovies sticking to the pan. Anchovies should gradually dissolve - if necessary, help the anchovies to dissolve by slowing crushing with a wooden spoon. Add 2-3 tablespoons olive oil, cook for 10 minutes on a medium to low heat. 1 to 2 minutes before removing the pan, add the butter, stir well.

Allow to slightly cool. Serve direct from the pan, or place the pan on the table and dig in as if it were a cheese fondu.

Preparation time: 15-20 minutes
Cooking time: 50-60 minutes

PIPERADE (***)

A Basque dish which can be served as an entrée or as a main dish.

> 2 TO 3 PERSONS
> 4 GREEN PEPPERS, CORE AND SEEDS REMOVED
> 1 SMALL ONION, FINELY CHOPPED
> 2 CLOVES GARLIC, FINELY CHOPPED
> 4 SMALL TO MEDIUM TOMATOES
> 3 EGGS
> 4 TO 6 SLICES RAW HAM (BAYONNE HAM IS BEST IF AVAILABLE)
> OLIVE OIL
> 2 TABLESPOONS FRESH SAGE, CHOPPED
> 2 TABLESPOONS FRESH ROSEMARY, CHOPPED
> 2 TABLESPOONS FRESH BASIL, CHOPPED
> PARSLEY, MINCED
> COOKING SALT, AND BLACK PEPPER

1) Wash the peppers, cut into large slices, remove seeds and cores, wash again. Now dice the peppers (cut into small strips).

2) Line the bottom of a wide pan with olive oil. Using a medium heat (not too hot), add the chopped onion, garlic, sage, rosemary and basil, and brown slowly. Then add the small pieces of peppers, stir well, and continue cooking all the contents on a medium heat for 40 to 50 minutes.

3) Wash the tomatoes, put them into boiling water for 1 or 2 minutes, and then remove the tomato skins. Mash the tomatoes and add to the pan about 15 minutes after the cooking process starts (tomatoes take less time to cook)

4) Beat 3 eggs in a bowl, add 3 pinches of cooking salt, add the minced parsley, a little black pepper, mix well, and pour into the pan 2 to 3 minutes before the cooking process is finished. Mix all the ingredients in the pan.

5) The ham is heated separately in a clean pan, lined with a thin layer of olive oil, heat slowly and add on top of your Piperade just before serving.

The Piperade should be served nice and hot.

Preparation time: 10-20 minutes
Cooking time: 15-20 minutes

SPINACH & SAGE (*)

2 PERSONS
700 G/ 1/2 LB FRESH SPINACH
1/2 ONION, FINELY CHOPPED & 1 CLOVE GARLIC ALSO FINELY CHOPPED
SAGE LEAVES, FINELY CHOPPED
20 G/1 OZ BUTTER
1/2 BROTH CUBE PREPARED APART IN 1/4 LITRE/8 FL OZ WATER
SALT AND PEPPER
GRATED CHEESE

1) Remove the spinach stalks. Carefully wash the spinach before cooking for 10 minutes in boiling salted water.

2) When cooked, strain and leave the spinach to cool. Squeeze out any water (best done with the hands).

3) Use a non-stick pan, and brown the onion, garlic, and sage (browning requires the right heat, not too hot, and not too little) - the butter, in this case, replaces oil for browning.

4) Lower the heat considerably, and when just warm, add the spinach, mix with the onion, garlic and sage. Now add the broth and stir slowly - add a little pepper. Just keep warm until serving, then strain and serve with grated cheese according to individual taste.

Preparation time: 20 minutes
Cooking time: 25-30 minutes

STUFFED POM-POMS (***)
(Peppers with a savoury stuffing)

2 PERSONS
2 RED OR YELLOW PEPPERS
150 G/5 OZ MINCED MEAT
50 G/2 OZ ITALIAN RAW HAM (JAMBON DE PARME)
2 TABLESPOONS GRATED CHEESE
1 CLOVE GARLIC, FINELY CHOPPED
1/2 MEDIUM ONION, FINELY CHOPPED
2 SPRIGS SAGE, FINELY CHOPPED
1/2 DL/2 FL OZ WHITE WINE
5 X 2 TABLESPOONS OIL (SUNFLOWER)
1 TEASPOON HERBES DE PROVENCE
2 SMALL ROUND PIECES BREAD
BLACK PEPPER AND SALT

1) First mix all the minced meat together with the ham (best done with the hands). Wash the peppers thoroughly. Cut a round opening at the top of each pepper, and remove all the insides (deseed and decore - all the white core and seeds are to be removed).

2) Take a grease-proof pan, fairly large with high sides. Add 4 or 5 tablespoons oil. When hot add the garlic, onion, sage, then the mincement and ham mixture. Add the herbs, pepper and pince of salt. Sauté on a brisk heat for approx. 5 minutes, turning the meat mixture in the process. Add the grated cheese at the end. This is the stuffing for the peppers.

3) Now proceed to fill the peppers with the stuffing, and block the openings with small round pieces of bread (otherwise the stuffing will fall out later).

4) Take the same saucepan. Add oil as required (3 tablespoons or more). Bring to a medium heat. Proceed to cook the stuffed peppers for 15 to 20 minutes. Add the white wine during the process.
Note that the peppers have to be placed horizontally into the pan, so that they cook on all sides. Occasionally, turn the peppers over. When the peppers are tender (check it with a sharp knife) you will know that the peppers are cooked and ready for serving (possibly with a salad).

Note: When cleaning the peppers use a very small spoon and a sharp knife, and avoid making too large an opening in the top of the peppers, or damaging the sides.

Preparation time: 60-95 minutes
Cooking time: 70 minutes

CELERY, BACON AND CHEESE CLANGER (***)

4 PERSONS
350-400 G/12-14 OZ CELERY (SIX LARGE STICKS OF CELERY)
175 G/6 OZ SMOKED BACON, DICED   100 G/4 OZ CHEDDAR CHEESE, GRATED
250 G/9 OZ SELF-RAISING FLOUR   125 G/4 1/2 OZ SHREDDED SUET (BEEF SUET)
2 TABLESPOONS OIL (SUNFLOWER)   1 TEASPOON SALT, BLACK PEPPER
1 EGG YOLK, BEAT (TO GLAZE THE ROLL BEFORE BAKING)
1 1/2 DL/ 1/4 PINT WATER   LITTLE BUTTER FOR GREASING THE BAKING TRAY
ABSORBENT KITCHEN PAPER

1) Mix the flour, suet, salt and pepper together in a large mixing bowl (a large salad bowl is ideal) - mix using a fork. Set aside.

2) Prepare the celery by removing any outer stalks, trim and wash. Boil in salted water for 20 minutes. Remove and allow to cool. Chop roughly into small parts (approx. 1 1/2 cm / 1/2" square). Use a shallow, wide frying pan. Heat the oil, and lightly fry the celery for 2 to 3 minutes.
Now add the chopped bacon. Continue to stir and fry on a medium heat for 5 minutes. Remove the celery and bacon to a plate on which you have placed a sheet of absorbent kitchen paper (to absorb the remaining oil and water).

3) Returning to your mixing bowl (1) - pour in the water slowly, and continue to mix until you have a stiff paste (use your floured hands to make the dough into a ball-like shape).
Place the dough on a lightly floured board (or any other surface suitable for rolling out the dough) and roll out into a rectangular shape of about 1/2 cm / 1/4" thick, and 24 cm / 9 1/2" wide. Length will be about 30 cm / 12" with the dough you have available.

4) Leave a border of about 2 1/2 cm / 1" down each long edge of the rolled out pastry. Spread the cheese over the entire surface of the pastry (leaving the edges free). Assist the cheese to sink into the pastry. Now add the bacon and celery over the cheese in a similar manner. Roll up the pastry tightly (lengthways) similar to a Swiss roll. Seal and secure the borders and edges by brushing with a little water.
Brush over the entire pastry roll with the yolk of one egg (to glaze) before placing the roll on the baking tray or sheet (which has first been greased with butter). Use a pre-heated oven (pre-heat for 10 minutes). Bake for 35 minutes at 180°C/350°F/Gas Mark 4. Serve hot.

Important: Avoid over-baking which would make the pastry too hard.

Preparation time: 15-20 minutes
Cooking time: 35-45 minutes

BROCCOLI FLAN (*)

2 TO 3 PERSONS
500 G/1 LB 2 OZ POTATOES
400 G/14 OZ BROCCOLI
1 LARGE TOMATO
100 G/4 OZ CHEDDAR CHEESE, GRATED
OREGANO
DRY ONION POWDER
PEPPER AND SALT
6 TABLESPOONS OIL (SUNFLOWER)

1) Cook the potatoes for 20 minutes in salted water, after first peeling, washing, and slicing into halves - allow to cool.

2) Prepare the broccoli, removing the stalks and retaining the florettes - wash, and cook in salted water for 15 minutes - allow to cool.

3) Place the tomato in boiling water to facilitate removing the skin - remove the core, and mash.

4) Mash the potatoes, mash the broccoli, and now mix together with the tomato (already mashed) - add the grated cheese, oregano, onion powder, pepper and salt. Continue mixing well until the tomato is absorbed and the entire mixture becomes solid.

5) Line a shallow wide stick-proof pan with oil - when hot add the mixture (use a pan which is slightly smaller than a large plate) - cover with a lid. At first a high heat and than medium. As soon as the underside is brown, slide on to a plate, reverse and slide back into the pan so that both sides are cooked (about 5 minutes each side).
When slightly brown on both sides remove and keep hot. Now prepare the remainder of the mixture in the same way using more oil as necessary.

Note: Browning the mixture in 2 stages avoids having too much mixture in the pan which is difficult to handle in terms of reversing, etc.

Preparation time: 10 minutes
Cooking time: 60 minutes

BAKED POTATOES (*)

2 PERSONS
COUNT ABOUT 225 G/ 1/2 LB POTATOES PER PERSON
10 G/ 1/2 OZ BUTTER
SALT

1) First scrub the potatoes. Make a small cross on the potatoes so that they do not burst in the oven. Do not peel.

2) Cover the bottom of a baking tin with alu foil.
Sprinkle salt over the potatoes. Place them on to the baking tin. Add a pat of butter on top of each potato.

3) Bake at 200°C/400°F/Gas Mark 6 in the centre of a pre-heated oven. Bake for one hour (until tender).

Preparation time: 10 minutes
Cooking time: 15-30 minutes

BOILED POTATOES WITH PARSLEY (*)

2 PERSONS
450 G/1 LB POTATOES
10 G/ 1/2 OZ BUTTER
PARSLEY
1 TEASPOON SALT

1) Wash the potatoes, peel, and wash them again before putting them into boiling salted water. Cooking time depends on the size of the potatoes - count 10 to 15 minutes for really small potatoes; larger potatoes count 20 to 30 minutes. One usually cuts large potatoes into halves to reduce the cooking time. Use a lid to cover the saucepan.

2) The parsley should be minced, or finely chopped, and then sprinkled over the potatoes only when they are cooked and strained. Add a small piece of butter to the hot potatoes before serving.

Preparation time: 10 minutes
Cooking time: 45 minutes

ROAST POTATOES (*)

2 PERSONS

1) Wash, peel and cut into halves. Boil in salted water for approx. 8 minutes. Strain and dry. Place in the baking tin around the meat roast and occasionally cover the potatoes with the meat juices (basting). Cooking time about 45 minutes.

Preparation time: 10-15 minutes
Cooking time: 40 minutes

MASHED POTATOES WITH SAUSAGES & ONIONS (**)

(good old "Sausages and Mash")

2 TO 3 PERSONS
5 TO 6 POTATOES, UNPEELED & WASHED (APPROX. 425 G/1 LB)
4 SMALL ONION (APPROX. 50 G/2 OZ)
250 G/9 OZ SMALL PORK SAUSAGES (ENGLISH SAUSAGES, IF POSSIBLE)
4 TABLESPOONS OIL (SUNFLOWER)
15 G/ 1/2 OZ BUTTER
1 DL/ 4 FL OZ MILK
1 TO 1.25 LITRES/1 3/4 TO 2 1/4 PINTS WATER (FOR THE POTATOES)
SALT AND PEPPER

1) Bring the water to a boil, add the potatoes (do not peel). Put a lid on the saucepan, and cook for 25 to 30 minutes (check whether cooked by putting in a knife to make sure the centres are soft - cooking time depends on the size of the potatoes).

2) Remove the potatoes when cooked, and peel (peeling very hot potatoes is easy once you know how - just hold the potatoes on a fork, and peel with an ordinary kitchen knife).
After peeling place the potatoes into a clean saucepan over a low heat (just to keep the potatoes hot). Mash using a large fork, add milk and butter so that you have nice mash (not too liquid). Add salt and pepper. Continue to keep hot.

3) Chop the onions and gently heat and brown in a non-stick pan using a little oil (cover the frying pan). When the onions start to turn brown add the sausages and fry, turning up the heat. Add a little more oil as necessary.

Serve when the sausages are cooked and brown, pouring the sauce from the sausages and onions over the potatoes (which you have served first).

Preparation time: 10-15 minutes
Cooking time: 35-40 minutes

RÖSTI (**)

2 PERSONS
450 G/1 LB POTATOES
2 TABLESPOONS OIL
20 G/1 OZ BUTTER
1 TEASPOON SALT X 2
PEPPER (BLACK)

1) First wash the potatoes, boil (unpeeled) in salted water for 20 to 25 minutes. Drain off the water and allow the potatoes to cool. Peel and grate. Add a little butter to the potatoes.

2) Heat the oil in a shallow frying pan, add the grated potatoes so as to cover the entire pan (level off). Season with salt and black pepper.

3) Commence frying on a high to medium heat and then lower the heat. Then invert the mixture so as to brown the potatoes on the other side. To have the potatoes nice and brown we need from 5 to 7 minutes (use a medium to low heat).

Serve nice and hot.

Note: Add more oil as necessary.

Preparation time: 20 minutes
Cooking time: 45-55 minutes

CAULIFLOWER & CHEESE SAVOURY (**)

2 TO 3 PERSONS (IF SERVED BEFORE OR AFTER A MAIN DISH IT WILL SERVE 4 TO 6 PERSONS)
1 LARGE CAULIFLOWER
4 TO 6 BACON RASHERS, CHOPPED
1/2 LARGE ONION, FINELY CHOPPED
2 SMALL TO MEDIUM TOMATOES
50 G/2 OZ GRATED CHEESE
3 TABLESPOONS OIL (SUNFLOWER)
ROSEMARY
SALT AND PEPPER

SAUCE
4 1/2 DL/ 3/4 PINT MILK   40 G/1 1/2 OZ BUTTER
40 G/1 1/2 OZ PLAIN FLOUR   50 G/2 OZ GRATED CHEESE
SEASONING (SALT AND PEPPER)

1) Commence by preparing the cauliflower cut away outer leaves and stalks, trim into small florettes wash. Cook in boiling salted water for 20 minutes (until tender).
Drain off all the water after the cauliflower is cooked and arrange in an ovenproof dish (grease the dish first with a little butter to avoid sticking).

2) Take a shallow frying pan and line the bottom with oil. Sear the bacon (diced) and slightly brown the finely chopped onions. Sprinkle the bacon and onions over the cauliflower.
Now proceed to remove the tomato skins (dip into boiling water to easily remove the skins). Cut away the stalks, cores and seeds - chop the remaining parts and spread over the contents in the ovenproof dish. Add a little salt and pepper as well as the rosemary. Sprinkle the grated cheese over the top.

3) Sauce - First melt the butter slowly over a medium heat.
Add the flour and cook for 2 minutes. Remove from the heat and add the milk slowly, gently stirring all the time. Place back over a medium heat and bring slowly to a boil allowing the contents to cook for a few minutes (continue to stir slowly). Add salt and pepper. Lower the heat to a simmer, continuing to stir until the mixture thickens and becomes smooth. Add the grated cheese and continue to stir.
Now pour the sauce over the ingredients in the dish.
Bake in a pre-heated (10 minutes) oven at 200°C/400°F/Gas Mark 6 for 20 minutes until the top becomes a golden brown colour.

Preparation time: 20 minutes
Cooking time: 55-60 minutes

SAVOURY GREEN BEANS (**)

(Al modo mia nonna)

2 PERSONS
400 G/14 OZ FRENCH GREEN BEANS
1/2 LARGE ONION, FINELY CHOPPED
3 TABLESPOONS OIL (SUNFLOWER)
2 GARLIC CLOVES, FINELY CHOPPED
2 TABLESPOONS TOMATO PURÉE
1 DL/4 FL OZ RED WINE
1 DL/4FL OZ MEAT BROTH (OR USE 1/2 MEAT BROTH CUBE)
FRESH BASIL
SALT AND PEPPER

1) Trim and taper the green beans (remove tops and tails) and wash. Allow the beans to dry using a strainer.
Cut the beans into halves.

2) Mix the tomato purée with the red wine. Prepare the meat broth.

3) Line a wide frying pan with oil, heat, and slightly brown the onion and garlic.

4) Step up the heat and add the beans to the pan. Mix the beans in the oil and continue to stir around. Lower the heat and slowly pour the red wine/tomato purée mixture into the pan, continue to stir. Increase the heat again for a few minutes and continue to stir.
Reduce the heat to medium and allow the beans to cook for 45 minutes to 1 hour (depends on the quality of the beans). Taste occasionally. Season with salt and pepper.
The beans should really stew in little liquid. As the liquid evaporates slowly add the meat broth making sure also that you do not have too much liquid in the pan.

Add the basil toward the end of the cooking process.

There should be hardly any liquid remaining at the end.

Note: All a question of carefully watching the heat and not having too much liquid in the pan at any time.

EASY EXCELLENT COOKING GUIDE

MEAT DISHES AND POULTRY

BRITISH AND EUROPEAN COOKING AT ITS BEST

Preparation time: 20-25 minutes
Cooking time: 70-90 minutes

BAKED MASHED POTATOES WITH MINCED BEEF (***)

3 TO 4 PERSONS (FR. "HACHIS PARMENTIER")
600 G/1 1/4 LB POTATOES   1/2 LITRE/18 FL OZ WATER (APPROX.)
1 TEASPOON SALT (FOR COOKING THE POTATOES)
40 G/ 1 1/2 OZ BUTTER   1 DL/4 FL OZ MILK
1 TEASPOON NUTMEG, GRATED   2 TABLESPOONS PARSLEY, FINELY CHOPPED
250 G/9 OZ STEWING BEEF, FINELY CHOPPED (MINCED)
3 SMALL ONIONS, FINELY CHOPPED
1 DL/4 FL OZ WHITE WINE   4 TABLESPOONS OIL (SUNFLOWER)
FRESH THYME   10 G/ 1/2 OZ BUTTER
1 TABLESPOON BREAD CRUMBS   SALT AND BLACK PEPPER

1) Commence by greasing an ovenproof dish with a little butter, and set aside.

2) Wash the potatoes, peel, wash again, and cut them into equal parts (see also page 87). Cook in salted boiling water. Count about 20 minutes cooking time (cover the saucepan with a lid).

3) When cooked, drain off the water and replace the potatoes into an empty saucepan over a very low heat. Mash the potatoes adding butter and milk in the process (add the milk slowly). Add half of the parsley and mix into the mashed potatoes together with a little grated nutmeg. Season with salt and pepper. Set the mashed potatoes aside.

4) The Meat - Line the bottom of a wide frying pan with oil, heat, and add the minced meat. Sear the meat well over a high heat. Add the chopped onions and stir. Lower the heat and stir in the remainder of the parsley - add pepper and salt. Gradually pour in the white wine. Increase the heat so that the meat is slowly cooking (and the liquid is evaporating). Add the remainder of the white wine. Lower the heat and allow the meat to continue cooking (total time for processing the meat is approximately 10 to 15 minutes). Now remove the pan and allow the contents to cool (you should have just a little liquid remaining).

5) Spread a layer of mashed potatoes into the bottom of the ovenproof dish. Now spread the meat with any liquid remaining. Sprinkle the fresh thyme over the meat. Add a top layer of mashed potatoes. Finally add a few butter flakes or knobs of butter on top of the potatoes. Lightly sprinkle the breadcrumbs over the top before placing into a pre-heated oven (pre-heat for 10 minutes) at 180°C/350°F/Gas Mark 4 for 40 minutes, and 200°C/400°F/Gas Mark 6 for 10 minutes, until the top is fairly brown (total oven time is 50 to 60 minutes).

Preparation time: 15 minutes
Cooking time: 15-20 minutes

BEEF & MORTADELLA HAMBURGERS (*)

2 PERSONS
300 G/11 OZ MINCED BEEF
70 G/3 OZ MORTADELLA SAUSAGE, MINCED (ITALIAN SAUSAGE FROM BOLOGNA)
2 TABLESPOONS OIL (SUNFLOWER)
PARSLEY, MINCED (1 TABLESPOON WHEN MINCED)
MIXED HERBS "HERBES DE PROVENCE"
SALT AND PEPPER

1) Mix the Mortadella with the minced beef (have your butcher mince the beef and the Mortedella, and mix both together).

2) Season with salt and pepper, parsley and "herbes de provence" (not too much salt because Mortadella is already salty).

3) Prepare the meat into shape with your hands, making four small to medium hamburgers.

4) Heat oil in a frying pan, and when the oil is hot put the meat in the pan and cook for about 5 minutes on each side. Serve hot (cooking time will vary according to how well done you like your meat).

Preparation time: 5-10 minutes
Cooking time: 10-15 minutes

BEEF STEAKS WITH "HERBES DE PROVENCE" (*)

2 PERSONS
250-300 G/9-11 OZ (2 SLICES) BEEF STEAKS (RUMP-STEAK, BEEF FILLETS OR SIRLOIN STEAK, OR OTHER SIMILAR SLICES OF MEAT)
3 TABLESPOONS OLIVE OIL
"HERBES DE PROVENCE" *

1) Pour the olive oil into a large plate and dip the steaks into the oil (so that the meat is covered and absorbs the oil).
   Sprinkle the herbs ("herbes de provence") over both sides of the steaks.

2) Heat a large shallow frying pan (grease-proof) so that the pan becomes very hot. Place the steaks into the pan. Turn so that the meat cooks on both sides.
   Cooking time will depend on the thickness of the meat and taste - count 3 to 4 minutes for medium done steaks.

Note: The above process helps to retain the flavour and taste of the meat.

* "Herbes de provence" = a French term meaning a mixture of herbs (fresh or dry): usually made up of thyme, rosemary, tarragon, oregano and marjoram.

Preparation time: 15 minutes
Cooking time: 30-40 minutes

BROCCOBURGERS (**)

3 TO 4 PERSONS
300 G/3/4 LB BEEF, MINCED
150 G/5 OZ SAUSAGE (PORK) MEAT, MINCED - SKIN REMOVED
(HAVE THE TWO MINCED TOGETHER AT TIME OF PURCHASE)
250 G/ 1/2 LB BROCCOLI
2 EGGS
50 G/2 OZ BREADCRUMBS (FINE)
FRESH BASIL, FINELY CHOPPED (2 TABLESPOONS)
FRESH THYME, FINELY CHOPPED
FRESH PARSLEY, FINELY CHOPPED (2 TABLESPOONS)
4 TABLESPOONS OIL (SUNFLOWER)
SALT AND PEPPER

1) Have the meat and sausage minced together by your butcher. Place the mince into a large mixing bowl.

2) After having removed the hard stalks from the broccoli, separate the florets into smaller units, wash, and cook for 15 minutes. Allow to cool before mashing and adding to the meat mixture (1).

3) Add the eggs (complete) the basil, parsley and thyme (all finely chopped) and the breadcrumbs.

4) Mix all the ingredients in the bowl (using your hands). After thoroughly mixing, make small round meatballs with the mixture.

5) Heat the oil in a shallow pan (brisk heat to start with) put in the meatballs and cook for 10 minutes, turning them over at intervals so that they cook on all sides. After 10 minutes reduce the heat and cook for a further 5 minutes (total cooking time 15 minutes).

Best served with a salad or a potato dish.

Preparation time: 30 minutes
Cooking time: 60 minutes

CORNISH PASTIES (***)

2 TO 4 PERSONS
300 G/11 OZ PUFF PASTRY OR SIMILAR READY-MADE "PÂTE FEUILLETÉE"
200 G/7 OZ RUMP STEAK, OR STEWING BEEF ("RAGOUT DE BŒUF") DICED (CUT INTO SMALL SQUARES OR FLAKES BY YOUR BUTCHER)
1 LARGE TURNIP, KOHLRABI, OR SWEDE
3 MEDIUM POTATOES
1 MEDIUM ONION, FINELY CHOPPED
3 SPRIGS OF BASIL
SALT AND BLACK PEPPER
FLOUR (FOR ROLLING OUT THE DOUGH)

Utensils: open baking flan tin, about 30 cm in diameter (grease first to avoid the pasties sticking to the tin)

With the above ingredients you will have 4 portions (4 pasties) The secret in making good pasties is to keep them nice and small. The tendency is to make the pasties too large. The Swede, if in season, is my choice.

1) Peel, wash and dice the potatoes, turnip (or swede, kohlrabi). Finely chop the onion.

2) Roll out the dough (if not pre-rolled) and cut into rounds of approx. 19 cm/7 1/2 inches in diameter, or smaller. (Remember to sprinkle a little flour on the board before rolling out your dough)

3) Mix the meat, potatoes and vegetables evenly into portions. Sprinkle the portions with basil. Add a little salt and black pepper. Place each portion on to a separate round of dough (the meat should be in the centre between the potatoes and vegetables - the juice of the meat will then penetrate).

4) Wet the edges of the dough, close the round carefully over the ingredients so that the dough remains firmly closed. Try giving the edges of the dough a decorative shape.

5) Heat the oven for 15 minutes at 220°C/450°F/Gas Mark 8. Cook for 45 minutes on 180°C/350°F/Gas Mark 4.

Note: Cornish pasties are really excellent. Not always easy for the first time, and you may well have to experiment. As a novelty starter you will have enough for 4 persons.

Preparation time: 15 minutes
Cooking time: 25 minutes

FLORENTINE HAMBURGERS (**)
(It. Polpettine alla Fiorentina)

2 PERSONS
250 G/ 1/2 LB MINCED MEAT (LEAN BEEF) - HAVE THE MEAT MINCED BY YOUR BUTCHER
2 EGGS
1 1/2 TABLESPOONS GRATED CHEESE
1/2 SMALL ONION, MINCED
1 CLOVE GARLIC, MINCED
1/2 GLASS WHITE WINE
2 TO 3 TABLESPOONS FINE BREADCRUMBS
FRESH THYME, PARSLEY, BASIL, MINCED
SALT AND PEPPER
3 TO 4 TABLESPOONS OLIVE OIL

1) Use a large mixing bowl. Mix the minced meat with the eggs, grated cheese, onion, garlic, thyme, parsley, basil, salt and pepper.
Mould into shape (square or round) and roll or cover with the breadcrumbs.

2) Pour 3 or 4 tbsp olive oil into shallow non-stick frying pan, heat (not too hot). Place the mixture into the pan and cook over a medium to low heat for 20 minutes. Turn occasionally so all sides are cooked. Prior to the end of the cooking process add the white wine (or earlier if the pan becomes too dry).

Serve hot, but they can also be eaten cold.

Preparation time: 20-30 minutes
Cooking time: 1 hr. 10-1 hr-40

IRISH STEW (***)

3 TO 4 PERSONS
600 G/1 1/4 LB LAMB FOR ROASTING (SHOULDER) DICED, (BONES REMOVED)
300 G/11 OZ CELERIAC (2 SMALL CELERIACS)   150 G/5 OZ GREEN BEANS
4 TO 6 MEDIUM POTATOES   3 CARROTS
2 MEDIUM ONIONS, CUT INTO HALVES   1 SMALL ONION, FINELY CHOPPED
2 CLOVES GARLIC, FINELY CHOPPED
1 LITRE/1 3/4 PINTS BROTH (2 MEAT BROTH CUBES)
3 TABLESPOONS OIL (SUNFLOWER)   2 DL/7 FL OZ RED WINE
FRESH THYME   } USE DRY IF FRESH NOT AVAILABLE
FRESH ROSEMARY
BLACK PEPPER   1 1/2 TABLESPOONS COOKING SALT

1) Commence by preparing all the vegetables: peel, wash and slice the potatoes into quarters or halves (depending on size). Peel the celeriacs, wash and slice into small parts. Taper the beans (cut off the ends) cut into two and wash. Peel, wash the carrots, cut into small slices.

2) Place all the vegetables (1) into boiling salted water and cook for 20 minutes. Cover the saucepan. When cooked drain off the water and set the vegetables aside.

3) Line a pan with a very thin layer of oil. When hot add the chopped onion and garlic. Add the meat (diced or small lumps) and sauté for a few minutes on both sides. Remove the pan from the heat and transfer all the meat, onions, garlic to an ovenproof tray (roasting tin or dish). Now add the onions which you have previously cut into halves.
Sprinkle the thyme and rosemary over the meat. Add a little pepper. Pour 1/2 litre/approx. 1 pint of broth into the ovenproof tin. Add 1 dl/4 fl oz red wine. Place in a preheated oven at 180°C/350°F/Gas Mark 4 and cook for 1 hr. 15 mins.

4) 45 minutes prior to the meat being cooked open the oven and add all the vegetables (2). Add a little pepper and salt, thyme and rosemary. The tendency is for the juices and gravy to dry. The vegetables and meat should be at least half covered by the gravy - if not add another 1/2 litre/about 1 pint of broth plus 1 dl/4 fl oz red wine Replace into the oven and continue the cooking process. Continue to check from time to time that there is enough liquid surrounding all the vegetables and meat [this is important]. Check for taste 15 minutes before the end.

Note: Use good red wine (avoid low grade cooking wine). Use vegetables and meat which are available even though it may not be a traditional Irish Stew.

Preparation time: 15-20 minutes
Cooking time: 2 hours

LANCASHIRE HOT-POT (***)

(A Good Old-English Dish)

> 2 TO 3 PERSONS
> 600 G/1 1/4 LB LAMB CHOPS (7 TO 8 CHOPS)
> 4 TO 5 LARGE POTATOES
> 1 1/2 OR 2 LARGE ONIONS
> SALT (APPROX. 2 TEASPOONS)
> PEPPER
> 4 DL 3/4 PINT MEAT BROTH (1 CUBE)
> FRESH THYME OR DRY

1) Wash the potatoes, peel, slice very thin. Peel the onions, and slice thin.

2) Prepare 3 to 4 dl/about 3/4 pint water and add a meat broth cube to the boiling water, and allow to boil until the cube has dissolved. Set aside.

3) Space the lamb chops in an ovenproof roasting tray or tin, 3 or 4 chops at the bottom, cover with the onions, then the potatoes slices, add the remaining lamb chops, onions, and finish with a last layer of potatoes slices. Add your salt, pepper, thyme as you space the chops, onions and potatoes. Finally, pour the broth over the contents of the tray. Cover with a lid before placing in the oven.

4) Roast in the oven and allow approx. 2 hours at 180°C/ 350°F/Gas Mark 4. About 1/2 hour prior to the end, remove the lid so as to brown the potatoes.

Preparation time: 20-30 minutes
Cooking time: 1 hr. 20-1 hr. 55
Standing time: 30 minutes

MOUSSAKA (**)

4 PERSONS
450 G/1 LB LAMB, MINCED (E.G. SHOULDER WITH BONE REMOVED)
1 MEDIUM-SIZE ONION, CHOPPED   2 CLOVES GARLIC, CHOPPED
450 G/1 LB AUBERGINES, THINLY SLICED
225 G/ 1/2 LB TOMATOES, PEELED (OR CAN TOMATOES) CHOPPED
2 TABLESPOONS TOMATO PURÉE
* 300 G/11 OZ POTATOES, THINLY SLICED
2 TABLESPOONS FRESH PARSLEY   1 TABLESPOON FRESH THYME
FRESH SAGE   SALT AND PEPPER
1 DL/4 FL OZ WHITE WINE   5 TABLESPOONS OIL (SUNFLOWER)
BÉCHAMEL (SEE PAGE 20 AND USE THE VARIATION OUTLINED ON THE SAME PAGE)

* note that potatoes are not really essential. It reduces the preparation time without potatoes; on the other hand, Moussaka specialists do use potatoes.

1) Commence by washing, peeling, boiling the potatoes in salted water for 15 minutes (not completely cooked).

2) Prepare the aubergines by washing, and cutting into small slices adding salt - leave for 30 minutes so as to extract the water (you can assist this process by gently squeezing the aubergine slices). Now fry in oil until a they become a nice golden colour - set aside.

3) Add more oil to the pan: fry the onions and garlic until slightly brown. Add the minced lamb - stir and sear the meat. Now stir in the chopped tomatoes. puree, salt, pepper, thyme and parsley. Reduce the heat and allow to simmer for 20 minutes. Add the white wine during the cooking process.

4) Prepare your Béchamel which is explained in detail on page 20 (use the variation with egg, grated cheese and breadcrumbs).

5) Grease a casserole with a little butter and commence by putting down a thin layer of Béchamel to cover the bottom of your casserole. Now add the first layer of aubergine slices, the meat mixture and meat juices (drain off any excess fat); continue with a layer of thinly sliced potatoes. Finish with a layer of remaining aubergines, and cover the top with a thickish layer of Béchamel. Sprinkle the breadcrumbs over the top before placing in the oven (pre-heated for 10 minutes). Bake in oven (on the lowest level) at 180°C/350°F/Gas Mark 4, for 50 to 60 minutes.

Preparation time: 25-35 minutes
Cooking time: 1 hr. 30-1 hr. 40

ROAST PORK WITH HERBS (***)

(ideally served with potatoes, carrots, onions, tomatoes)

> 3 TO 4 PERSONS
> 700 G/1 1/2 LB PORK ROAST (OFF THE BONE, SUITABLE FOR ROASTING SUCH AS SHOULDER, LOIN, ETC.)
> 2 MEDIUM ONIONS, PEELED, CUT INTO HALVES
> 3 CLOVES GARLIC, CHOPPED
> 2 SPRIGS ROSEMARY, CHOPPED
> 2 TO 3 DL/7 FL OZ TO 1/2 PINT RED WINE
> OLIVE OIL
> 1 LITRE/1 3/4 PINTS BROTH (STOCK OR 1 BROTH CUBE)
> SALT AND PEPPER

1) Have your butcher pick out a nice small pork joint for roasting (without any bone). Vegetables are optional. You will need a baking tin, or oven-proof tray/dish (not too large).

2) First cut deep into the pork joint and fill in the slits with garlic, rosemary and other herbs of your choice.

3) Pre-heat the oven on 230°C/450°F/Gas Mark 8 for ten minutes.

4) In the meantime, pour a small quantity of olive oil into the baking tin and smear over all sides of the joint. Add the onions. Pour 2 to 3 dl/7 fl oz to 1/2 pint of red wine into the tin. Now place the joint (in the baking tin) into the oven at 180°C/350°F/Gas Mark 4 for approx. 1 1/2 hours (uncovered). Check out the time also with your butcher, too.

5) Occasionally check that the liquid round the joint is ample. Half way through roasting, or earlier, pour your stock or broth cube liquid over the joint (baste). Repeat if the joint becomes too dry.

6) When the joint is cooked turn off and allow it to remain in the heated oven for 10 minutes or so before serving.
Before carving (on a board) remember to remove any string or net (if the joint has been tied).

Note: To know if the meat is sufficiently roasted insert a sharp knife to see if tender, and if still pinkish and/or blood still runs you know that the meat is not fully cooked. Optional: Peel and wash the potatoes, carrots and boil in salted water for 10 minutes (cut the potatoes into halves, and slice the carrots before cooking). Transfer around the pork joint in the baking tin. Do this 45 minutes before the roast is done. Include the tomatoes at the same time. Suggestion: 6 potatoes, 2 carrots, 2 to 3 small tomatoes.

Preparation time: 15-20 minutes
Cooking time: 1 hr. 45 minutes

STEAK AND KIDNEY PIE (***)

4 PERSONS
500 G/1 LB 2 OZ STEWING BEEF, CUT INTO ABOUT 5 CM/2" CUBES
(USE CHUCK OR SIMILAR - FR. PALERON OR PALETTE)
350 G/12 OZ PIE CRUST PASTRY OR SHORTCRUST (FR. PÂTE BRISÉE)
1 MEDIUM ONION, FINELY CHOPPED
1/2 VEAL KIDNEY, SLICED
CARROTS AND 1 SMALL CELERY ROOT, CHOPPED (NOTE - CARROTS & CELERY ARE NOT ESSENTIAL)
BEEF STOCK (1/2 TO 3/4 LITRE - 1 TO 1 1/4 PINTS) OR USE
2 BROTH CUBES   1 TABLESPOON FLOUR
1/2 TEASPOON SALT, 1/4 TEASPOON PEPPER
FRESH OR DRY ROSEMARY   5 TABLESPOONS OIL (SUNFLOWER)
A LITTLE BUTTER FOR GREASING THE DISH

1) Brown the onion in the oil using a deep, wide saucepan (use a brisk heat). Add the meat and sear (to remove the redness)

2) Add the boiling stock. Cover the pan and allow the contents to low-boil for 1 hour until tender. After 30 minutes add the kidney, pepper, rosemary, salt and flour. Re-cover and continue on a low-boil for another 30 minutes.

3) In the meantime, roll out the pastry dough to the shape of your pie-dish. Leave a border of about 2 cm/1" so as to cover the edges of the pie-dish. (If you have no pie-dish available any ovenproof dish will do provided it has a similar shape to a pie, although even this is not absolutely essential). Do not overlook greasing the edges of the pie-dish with a little butter.

4) If you are using carrots and celery root, which I like to use, these should be prepared (peeled, washed and cut into small parts) and cooked separately in salted boiling water for 30 minutes (while the meat is stewing).

5) After one hour (when the meat is tender) remove the meat from the heat and allow to cool. Transfer the meat and broth to the ovenproof dish. Mix in the partially cooked carrots and celery root.

6) The only tricky part… stretch your pastry to cover the entire top of the pie-dish (including the contents). The borders of the pastry are to be folded over the sides of the dish. Slightly wet the pastry edges to easily stick them down. Lastly, make a small funnel-shape opening at the top of the pastry (to allow the steam to escape). Glaze the pastry over with the yolk of an egg. Place your pie into a pre-heated oven (pre-heat for 10 minutes) and bake for 30 to 35 minutes at 180°C/350°F/Gas Mark 4.

Preparation time: 15-20 minutes
Cooking time: 1 hr. 10-1 hr. 25

SWISS SHEPHERD'S PIE (***)

3 OR 4 PERSONS
300 G/11 OZ BEEF, MINCED (USE STEWING BEEF OR RAGOUT)
150 G/5 OZ SAUSAGE MEAT (PORK) REMOVE SKIN
500 G/1 LB 2 OZ POTATOES FOR BOILING)
250 G/9 OZ TOMATOES   1 MEDIUM ONION, FINELY CHOPPED
2 CLOVES GARLIC, FINELY CHOPPED   3 TBS PARSLEY, FINELY CHOPPED
1 TABLESPOON NUTMEG
5 PLUS 2 TABLESPOONS OIL (SUNFLOWER)
2 TEASPOONS DRIED OREGANO (OR FRESH IF AVAILABLE)
20 G/1 OZ BUTTER   SALT AND BLACK PEPPER

Note: First have your butcher mince the beef and sausage meat together for you (remember to discard the sausage skin)

1) Peel the potatoes and boil in salted water until cooked (refer to the recipe on boiled potatoes). Drain off the water and place the potatoes into a bowl. Mash the potatoes, season with parsley. Add a sprinkling of nutmeg, salt and pepper. Put aside, and continue with other steps.

2) Peel and finely chop the onion and garlic. Place the tomatoes into boiling water for a minute or two in order to easily remove the skins. Once the skins removed mash the tomatoes.

3) Line the bottom of a large frying pan with a thin layer of oil. Heat, and when fairly hot add the minced meat and sausage mixture together with the oregano. The meat mixture has to become nicely brown, at which time transfer it to an ovenproof dish (which you will have greased with a little butter in the meantime).

4) Add a further one or two tbsp oil to the pan, bring back to medium heat, transfer the onions, garlic and mashed tomatoes into this pan and continue to stir slowly until almost liquid. Season with salt and black pepper. Remove from the heat and mix into the meat mixture (3) - mix well.

5) Now add the mashed potatoes (1) evenly over the contents of the ovenproof dish (the mashed potatoes have to cover the other ingredients). Sprinkle butter flakes over the potatoes.

6) Cook in the oven on 180°C/350°F/Gas Mark 4 for 50 to 60 minutes, until the top becomes a golden brown colour.

Note: Ideal side-dish - why not a variety of vegetables which you just heat (not cook). Place them in the oily (empty) frying pan, add a little butter, season, bring to a brisk heat, In a jiffy this will be ready when your pie comes out of the oven.

Preparation time: 15-25 minutes
Cooking time: 25-35 minutes

TOURNEDOS EN CROÛTE (***)

2 PERSONS
2 TOURNEDOS (FILLET STEAKS) APPROX. 175 G/6 OZ EACH
200 G/7 OZ PUFF OR HOT WATER CRUST PASTRY
50 G/2 OZ LIVER PÂTÉ
20 G/1 OZ BUTTER
2 TABLESPOONS SHERRY
1 EGG, BEATEN
2 SPRIGS FRESH THYME
SALT AND PEPPER

1) First melt the butter in a flat frying pan. Brown or sauté the meat on each side for about 1 or 2 minutes.

2) Roll out your pre-prepared dough to make 2 squares (each large enough to cover a tournedos).

3) When the tournedos are cool, add the thyme, salt and pepper, cover with a light layer of liver pâté (use the sherry to soften the pâté).

4) Beat one egg separately and set aside.

5) Wrap the dough around each tournedos making sure the ends are closed. If you are able to decorate the pasties with surplus dough this adds to the appeal.
Brush the pasties with the beaten egg (4) to give a glossy coating.

6) Place the pasties in a pre-heated oven and bake for 25 to 30 minutes (until the pasties are nice and brown) using 200°C/400°F/Gas Mark 6.

Suggestion: Serve with peas and/or carrots, together with a salad.

Preparation time: 10 minutes
Cooking time: 15 minutes

VEAL CUTLETS WITH MARSALA (**)

2 PERSONS
400 G/14 OZ VEAL CUTLETS (2 CUTLETS) OR MORE
1 MEDIUM ONION, FINELY CHOPPED (20-30G/1 - 1 1/2 OZ)
4 TABLESPOONS OIL (SUNFLOWER)
3 TO 4 SPRIGS SAGE, FINELY CHOPPED
1/2 DL/2 FL OZ MARSALA
1/2 TEASPOON SALT
BLACK PEPPER

1) Line the bottom of a large non-stick frying pan with oil. Add the finely chopped onion, sage, and brown on a brisk heat. Remove the onion, sage, and remains of the oil to a small clean plate.

2) Your pan is still hot and oily. Now add the cutlets (add more oil if necessary) fry on a high heat for 2 to 3 minutes only, lower the heat and allow to cook through for 5 minutes becoming brown on both sides. Add more oil to the pan if too dry.

3) Before the cutlets are ready for serving, replace the sage, onion, and oil (1) back into the pan, mix well with cutlets. Pour 1/2 dl/2 fl oz Marsala over the contents of the pan, add salt and pepper.

Serve hot.

Preparation time: 15 minutes
Cooking time: 50-60 minutes
Standing time: 30 minutes

VEAL STEW A LA PARISIENNE (***)

2 PERSONS
400 G/14 OZ VEAL STEWING MEAT, CUT INTO MEDIUM SIZE PIECES. ADD A SMALL PIECE OF VEAL TROTTER IF AVAILABLE
1 MEDIUM ONION, CHOPPED
GARLIC AND TARRAGON } DRY, SPRINKLE
1 BAYLEAF
2 CLOVES
50 G/2 OZ MUSHROOMS, DRY (SOAK BEFOREHAND ABOUT 30 MINUTE)
1 TEASPOON BUTTER
1 TEASPOON PLAIN FLOUR
5 TABLESPOONS OIL (SUNFLOWER)
1/2 DL/2 FL OZ WHITE WINE
1 TABLESPOON TOMATO KETCHUP
1 BROTH CUBE (MEAT) OR STOCK IF AVAILABLE
1 TEASPOON COGNAC
SALT AND PEPPER

1) Prepare a broth cube (meat) in 1/2 dl/2 fl oz boiling water (if no stock available) and set aside.

2) Line the saucepan with oil, bring to a high heat, put in the veal pieces with the small piece of trotter, and brown on all sides for 5 to 10 minutes.

3) Lower heat, add all the ingredients (onion, garlic, tarragon, bayleaf, cloves, mushrooms, broth, ketchup, white wine, 3/4 tablespoon cooking salt, and cook on a low heat for 40 to 50 minutes. Stir occasionally, and add more wine, or a little water if too dry.

4) Separately, prepare 1 teaspoon butter with 1 teaspoon flour and mix together, add to the source towards the end of the cooking process.

The cognac is added last after you have removed the stew from the heat - give a final good stir before serving.

Preparation time: 10-15 minutes
Cooking time: 10-15 minutes

CHICKEN LIVERS WITH MARSALA (**)

"Petits foies de volailles au Marsala"

2 PERSONS
450 G/1 LB SMALL CHICKEN LIVERS
10 G/1/2 OZ BUTTER
2 SMALL ONIONS, FINELY CHOPPED
6 TABLESPOONS OIL [SUNFLOWER]
SAGE, CHOPPED
1 TEASPOON SALT
1 DL/4 FL OZ MARSALA

1) Line the bottom of a frying pan with oil and bring to a brisk heat. Place the chopped onions, sage and butter into the pan.

2) As soon as the contents of the pan start to become brown add the chicken livers, stir well, and cover with a lid. The chicken livers have to cook until no longer red.

3) When the chicken livers are cooked on all sides (repeat, no longer red) lower the heat, remove the pan from the heat for moment while you pour in the Marsala. Now place the pan back over a low heat, continue to stir well. Add your salt.

Entire cooking process should not take more than seven to ten minutes.

Rapid solution for vegetables

Example: Take a tin of pre-cooked mixed carrots and peas. Just heat (not cook). Drain off the liquid. Return the vegetables to the saucepan and add 10 g butter, a little garlic and onion, re-heat and stir well.

Preparation time: 10-15 minutes
Cooking time: 20 minutes

CHICKEN LIVER PATE (***)

(It. Crostini di Fegatini)

4 PERSONS
300 G/11 OZ SMALL CHICKEN LIVERS
1 SMALL ONION, CHOPPED
SAGE LEAVES
1 CLOVE GARLIC, CHOPPED
4 TABLESPOONS OLIVE OIL
1 TIN ANCHOVIES (6 TO 8 FILLETS)
2 DL/7 FL OZ CHICKEN BROTH (1/2 BROTH CUBE)
1/2 TABLESPOON PLAIN FLOUR
2 TO 3 TABLESPOONS MARSALA

1) Line a frying pan with 2 tablespoons olive oil and heat. When hot add the onion, sage and garlic. When brownish, remove and place on a separate plate.

2) Separately, prepare 2 dl/7 fl oz broth (using chicken broth cubes, assuming we have no stock available).

3) Add a further 1 to 2 tablespoons olive oil into the same pan. First sauté the chicken livers, cover the pan, turn the livers occasionally. Lower heat, add the onion, sage and garlic. Cook for 5 to 8 minutes. Towards the end add the flour and broth, stir and mix slowly.

4) When the chicken livers are cooked (should be soft, and brownish on all sides - no blood visible) add the anchovies and Marsala. Mix and stir. Allow to cool for a few minutes.

5) Run the chicken livers (including the broth) slowly through a food processor or electric mixer until you have a nice pâté. If too dry, add the remainder of the broth to the pâté.

Place in the refrigerator ready for serving cold, with hot toast.

Preparation time: 15-20 minutes
Cooking time: 1 hr. 20 minutes

GUINEA FOWL, ROASTED (**)

(Fr. Pintade Rôtie)

> 4 PERSONS
> 1.5 KG/3 1/4 LBS GUINEA FOWL - THE GUINEA FOWL SHOULD BE COMPLETELY PREPARED (THE INSIDE CLEANED OUT, AND TRUSSED) BY YOUR BUTCHER - YOU WANT YOUR BIRD OVEN-READY, OR ALMOST.
> 100 G/40 OZ PANCETTA, OR LEAN, STREAKY BACON
> 50 G/20 OZ BUTTER
> 6 TABLESPOONS OLIVE OIL
> FRESH THYME (A GOOD HANDFUL)
> COOKING SALT... 1 TABLESPOON

1) Commence by making a large knob of butter - place one tablespoon of salt into the centre of the butter.
   Stuff the butter into the main cavity of the Guinea Fowl (push it well in). Do the same with the thyme, pushing it well into the cavity.

2) Place the bird into a large, ovenproof tray. Smear oil over the bird, top and bottom. Cover it with pancetta or bacon slices. Now smear some more oil all over.

3) Pre-heat the oven for 10 minutes at 200°C/400°F/Gas Mark 6. Roast the Guinea Fowl for 1 hour 20 minutes at 190°C/375°F/Gas Mark 5. Remove the pancetta or bacon after 50 minutes. At this stage baste the bird thoroughly with all the fat and juices (in the roasting tray). Baste again some 10 minutes before removing it from the oven.
   It is important to baste the Guinea Fowl during the roasting. It necessary add more olive oil.

Note: The Guinea Fowl belongs to the same family as the pheasants. it is a native of West Africa.

Instead of presenting different poultry recipes I chose the Guinea Fowl as one example of roasting a bird in the oven, and particularly the Guinea Fowl because many prefer its unique taste; however, make very sure that it is not too dry when you remove it from the oven.

EASY EXCELLENT COOKING GUIDE

FISH

BRITISH AND EUROPEAN COOKING AT ITS BEST

Preparation time: 15-20 minutes
Cooking time: 30 minutes

SEA BASS, BAKED IN THE OVEN (**)

(Fr. Loup de mer, It. Spigola)

2 PERSONS
800 G-1 KG/2 LBS FRESH SEA BASS, SCALED, GUTTED, SPLIT & WASHED (HAVE YOUR FISHMONGER DO THIS)
2 TO 3 DL/7 FL OZ TO 1/2 PINT WHITE WINE (USE GOOD QUALITY)
HERBS CONSISTING OF FRESH THYME, DILL, ROSEMARY, AND PARSLEY
1 CLOVE GARLIC
5 TABLESPOONS OLIVE OIL
BLACK OLIVES, STONED
1/2 LEMON JUICE
SALT AND PEPPER
LEMON WEDGES

1) Commence by chopping (roughly) all the herbs and garlic. Pass these (together) through a mincer. Put aside.

2) Wash the sea bass again and dry. Place it into a roasting tin. pour the olive oil and lemon juice over the fish. Turn the fish over in the tin so that it soaks in the liquid.
   Add a little salt and pepper.
   Place the herbs and garlic mixture (1) into the fish cavities.
   Lastly, pour the white wine over the fish, add the black olives around the fish.

3) Pre-heat the oven for 10 minutes. Place your roasting tin containing the sea bass into the oven, at 180°C/350°F/Gas Mark 4 and leave for 25 to 30 minutes.
   After 15 minutes baste the fish (with the liquid in the tin). Turn the fish over. Continue the baking process.
   When the 25/30 minutes have elapsed the skin should come off easily. At this stage remove the fish from the oven.
   Cut the fish in half with a sharp knife to make 2 portions. Serve with lemon wedges.

Preparation time: 15 minutes
Cooking time: 30-40 minutes

PAN-BAKED TROUT (**)

(applicable to all types of Trout, Carp, Char or similar freshwater fish)

> 2 PERSONS
> 600 G/1 1/4 LB TROUT
> 1 SMALL ONION, FINELY CHOPPED
> 1 CLOVE GARLIC, FINELY CHOPPED
> 3 TABLESPOONS OLIVE OIL
> 1 DL/4 FL OZ WHITE WINE
> FRESH THYME, CHOPPED
> FRESH PARSLEY, CHOPPED
> DILL
> CHERVIL
> 20 G/1 OZ BUTTER
> 2 TEASPOONS COOKING SALT
> BLACK PEPPER
> LEMON WEDGES

1) Have the fish prepared at time of purchase. All you should need to do is to wash and dry (remove any fins if not already done)
Use a large ovenproof pan. Prepare all the ingredients (herbs, onions, garlic, etc.)

2) Stuff the cavities of he fish with these ingredients (1). Rub the outsides with butter. Place in the pan, add the salt and pepper, spoon the oil and wine over the fish.

3) Place in the oven and bake for 30 to 40 minutes on 180°C/350°F Gas Mark 4. Check occasionally and if too dry add another 1 dl/4 fl oz of white wine into the pan.

4) When serving add lemon wedges to each plate.

Suggestions for vegetables: Spinach served on a side-plate.

Preparation time: 10-15 minutes
Cooking time: 10-15 minutes

PERCH FILLETS (**)

2 TO 3 PERSONS
450 G/1 LB PERCH FILLETS
4 TABLESPOONS PLAIN FLOUR
2 LEMONS, CUT INTO WEDGES
1 TEASPOON SALT
4 TO 6 TABLESPOONS OIL (SUNFLOWER)

1) Wash and dry the fish before coating with a thin layer of flour.

2) Line a wide shallow, stick-proof frying pan with a thin layer of oil, and when the oil is hot (toss a small piece of onion into the oil to see if it sizzles) place your fillets into the pan and fry slowly. Heat control is very important, as well as making sure you have enough oil in the pan. Too hot and the perch will burn, and too low and they will not fry. Cover the frying pan with a protective screen to avoid the oil splashing.
When one side is brown, turn the fillets over and brown the other side. Add salt during the process.

3) Separately, have a heat-proof dish ready on a very low heat. Place a sheet of kitchen paper into the dish, and as the fillets are fried on both sides transfer them into this dish. The paper absorbs the fat, and the fillets remain warm.
In the meantime, add more oil to the pan if required and continue to fry the remaining fillets.
Serve hot with lemon wedges.

Preparation time: 15 minutes
Cooking time: 10-15 minutes

RED MULLET GRILLED (**)

2 PERSONS
650 G/1 LB 7 OZ RED MULLET (2 OR 3) - SCALED, SPLIT, GUTTED AND WASHED - HAVE YOUR FISHMONGER DO THIS
FRESH THYME (2 TO 3 TABLESPOONS)
FENNEL GRAINS (DRY)
2 CLOVES GARLIC, FINELY CHOPPED
4 TABLESPOONS OLIVE OIL
1/2 YOGHURT (PLAIN)
1/2 LEMON JUICE
1 TABLESPOON OIL (SUNFLOWER)
SALT AND PEPPER

1) First make grooves or slashes in the fish (both sides) at about 3 cm intervals. Smear olive oil all over the fish, and stuff garlic, fennel and thyme into the cavities. Smear the remainder of these ingredients over the fish.

2) Oil your rack. Preheat the grill for 5 minutes. Grill the fish on both sides for 6 to 8 minutes. Control and do not overcook.

3) Pour 1/2 yoghurt and 1/2 lemon juice into a small mixing bowl. Add a little olive oil, pepper and salt and beat. Serve this sauce separately on each plate. Lemon wedges are optional.

Preparation time: 15 minutes
Cooking time: 10-15 minutes

GRILLED SALMON WITH HERBS (**)

3 PERSONS (THESE ARE QUITE GENEROUS PORTIONS, BUT GRILLED FISH IS EXCELLENT)
600 G/1 1/4 LB (NET) FRESH SALMON STEAKS, SALMON CUTLETS OR SLICES
75 G/3 OZ BUTTER
2 TABLESPOONS FRESH CHERVIL OR DILL, MINCED
1 TABLESPOONS PARSLEY, MINCED
JUICE OF 1/2 OF ONE LEMON   2 TABLESPOONS OIL (SUNFLOWER)
SALT AND BLACK PEPPER   LEMON WEDGES
OPTIONAL: 4 TOMATOES, SMALL TO MEDIUM, WASHED AND HALVED
DRIED PARSLEY, GARLIC, ONION AND CELERY SALT (OR SIMILAR)
FOR SPRINKLING OVER THE TOP OF THE TOMATOES.

1) Have the salmon prepared for you at time of purchase so that you only have to wash and dry it before grilling. If you have chosen thick salmon slices, make narrow grooves or slashes at about 3 cm intervals to enable the heat to penetrate when the fish is grilling.

2) Lightly oil your grilling rack

3) Over a low heat, melt half of your butter in a small pan (keep half of the butter for later). Pour or brush the melted butter over the salmon (best done on a plate). Season with a little black pepper and salt. Retain some melted butter for later (5).

4) Put the tomatoes (with the garnish on top) on to your grilling rack; place the rack under the pre-heated grill - leave for about 4 to 5 minutes, then remove.

5) Now add the fish on to the grilling rack (with the tomatoes) and put the rack back under the grill. Grill for 3 to 4 minutes under a very hot grill. Halfway through the grilling (after 3 to 4 minutes) turn the fish over to the other side, pour more melted butter over the fish, place back under the grill for another 3 to 4 minutes. Take care not to over cook the fish. Keep it moist throughout the grilling process.

6) In the meantime, re-heat the pan and slowly melt the remainder of the butter. Mix in the lemon juice, minced chervil or dill, and parsley ; mix well and retain on a very low heat until serving your salmon.

Note: When the salmon is cooked (flesh should come apart when a sharp knife is inserted) remove to a serving dish and pour the sauce over the salmon. Have lemon wedges available for each plate.

Preparation time: 10-15 minutes
Cooking time: 10-15 minutes

FILLETS OF SOLE (**)

2 OR 3 PERSONS
4 TO 6 FILLETS OF SOLE (350 G-450 G/12 OZ-1 LB) - SKINNED, PREPARED AND CLEANED
4 TABLESPOONS PLAIN FLOUR
4 TABLESPOONS OIL (SUNFLOWER)
LEMON WEDGES
SALT

1) Dip the fish into plain flour to nicely coat.

2) Pour oil into a frying pan so that the bottom of the pan is lined with a thin layer (use a non-stick pan)

3) Heat the oil (not too hot - after a minute or so throw a small piece of onion into the pan to see if it begins to start sizzling). This is your sign to dip the fillets into the pan, and fry on both sides until becoming a golden brown colour. Step up the heat as necessary, but control so as not to burn the fillets of sole. If necessary add more oil. Use a protective screen cover (to avoid getting splashed with the oil).

From the time you place the fish into the hot oil it takes a total time of 10 to 15 minutes, and less if you use a higher heat.

Add a pinch of salt just before serving.

Serve hot with lemon wedges.

Preparation time: 5-10 minutes
Cooking time: 10-15 minutes

TROUT IN OLIVE OIL (*)

2 PERSONS
2 FRESH TROUT, MEDIUM SIZE 600 G/1 1/4 LB APPROX.
(PREPARED AND CLEANED AT TIME OF PURCHASE)
JUICE OF ONE LEMON
THYME ⎫
ONION ⎬ DRY
GARLIC ⎭
SALT AND PEPPER
1 BAYLEAF,
LEMON WEDGES

1) Add the salt, pepper, lemon juice, thyme, onion, garlic, bayleaf to the water which is then brought to a boil.

2) Place the trout into the boiling water, reduce the heat to a simmer and leave for 5 to 10 minutes (depending on size).

3) When cooked, remove skins, etc., and dress with olive oil; add lemon wedges to each plate.

Preparation time: 15-20 minutes
Cooking time: 40-45 minutes

SOLE BAKED IN THE OVEN (**)
(with potatoes)

2 PERSONS
600 G/1 1/2 LBS SOLE (2 OR 3)
450 G/1 LB POTATOES
1 MEDIUM-SIZED ONION, THINLY SLICED
2 CLOVES GARLIC, CHOPPED FINE
4-5 TABLESPOONS OLIVE OIL
2 DL/6 FL OZ WHITE WINE
10 G/1/2 OZ BUTTER
SALT AND PEPPER
FRESH THYME
DILL
LEMON WEDGES

1) Have the fish prepared by your supplier, including, if possible the removal of the dark skin, although not essential. Wash and dry before lightly dipping the fish into olive oil.

2) Use an ovenproof baking tray. Grease it with a little butter.

3) Boil the potatoes (peeled and washed) in salted water for 20 minutes.

4) Arrange the potatoes with the onions and garlic on the baking tray. Arrange the fish on the tray. Add the thyme, dill, salt and pepper. Add 2 dl white wine over the fish.

5) Pre-heat the oven for 10 minutes. Now bake for 20 to 25 minutes at 180°C/350° Gas Mark 4.

Serve with lemon wedges.

Preparation time: 10-15 minutes
Cooking time: 12-15 minutes

GRILLED SOLE WITH TOMATOES (**)

2 PERSONS
600-700 G/1 1/2 LBS SOLE (2 OR 3 LARGE SOLE IN THEIR SKINS)
6 SMALL TOMATOES, CUT INTO HALVES
5 TABLESPOONS OLIVE OIL
1/2 TO 1 TEASPOON PEPPER
2 TEASPOONS SALT
2 OR 3 BAY LEAVES
LEMON WEDGES

Have your supplier prepare the sole so that all you need do is to wash and dry the fish

1) Dip the fish into olive oil, and make sure your grill rack is wet with oil too. Season by sprinkling both sides of the fish with salt and pepper. Place the fish on the grill rack with the tomatoes (cut into halves) - place the tomatoes round the fish in the corners. Add the bay leaves.

2) Pre-heat your grill for 5 to 10 minutes, usually at maximum temperature. Place the grill rack or tray with the fish and tomatoes under the grill, and grill for 6 minutes on each side (total grilling time about 12 minutes).

When properly cooked the skin and flesh come away easily. Make sure you do not overcook.

Serve immediately with lemon wedges.

EASY EXCELLENT COOKING GUIDE

DESSERTS

BRITISH AND EUROPEAN COOKING AT ITS BEST

Preparation time: 15 minutes
Cooking time: 30-35 minutes

APPLE CRUMBLE (**)

3 TO 4 PERSONS
4 LARGE COOKING APPLES
4 TABLESPOONS CASTER SUGAR
1 TABLESPOON CINNAMON
4 TABLESPOONS BUTTER
3-4 TABLESPOONS FLOUR (WHITE, PLAIN)
RIND OF ONE LEMON, GRATED
JUICE OF 1 LEMON

1) Use an ovenproof receptacle such as a shallow cake or tart tin. Wash, peel and cut the apples into small slices.
Add the lemon juice and rind (grated). Add 2 tablespoons sugar and 2 knobs of butter.

2) Sprinkle the cinnamon over the apples. Pour one cup of water into the cake tin.

3) Using a mixing bowl proceed to place the flour, 2 tablespoons sugar, 2 tablespoons butter into the bowl and mix thoroughly.

4) Spread the contents of the bowl over the apple slices adding 2 more knobs of butter.

5) Pre-heat the oven for 10 minutes. Insert the apples in the tin into the oven and bake for 30 minutes on 180°C/350°F/Gas Mark 4.

Suggestion: Serve with custard or whipped cream.

Preparation time: 15-20 minutes
Cooking time: 40-50 minutes

APPLE TART (*)

3 TO 4 PERSONS
450 G/1 LB SHORTCRUST PASTRY ("PÂTE À GÂTEAU")
4 LARGE DESSERT APPLES
10 G/1/2 OZ BUTTER
1 TABLESPOON BROWN SUGAR
2 TO 3 TABLESPOONS FLOUR (FOR ROLLING OUT THE DOUGH)
OVENPROOF FLAN DISH OR TIN (APPROX. 30 CM / 12" IN DIAMETER)

1) Roll out your dough (if not prerolled) to fit a flat flan dish. First grease the dish with a little butter to avoid the dough sticking. Make lots of very small holes in the dough (using a fork) once the dough is in the dish.

2) Wash, peel and core the apples. Cut the apples into thin slices, and place the slices onto the dough so that the entire baking dish or tin is completely covered with the apple slices.

3) Place in the oven and bake for 40 to 50 minutes on 160°C/325°F/Gas Mark 3.
Just before the tart is baked, remove and sprinkle with brown sugar. and replace in oven.

Notes:

1) Essentially there are three different ways of preparing the dough - first, the easy way with prerolled dough, if available (this is a great time saver). With prerolled you need only stretch and cut it to shape (flour is not needed). Another possibility is to buy ready-made dough but you roll it out yourself to the shape desired.
The third way is, of course, to make your own dough.

2) After peeling the apples (to avoid the apples discolouring) put the slices first into lemon juice which you have first mixed with water.

3) Other fruit tarts can be made in exactly the same way (e.g. plums, greengages, apricots, etc.). More brown sugar is needed for juicy fruit which you sprinkle on before placing into the oven.

Preparation time: 10 minutes
Cooking time: 20 minutes

APPLE AND YOGURT DESSERT (*)

3 TO 4 PERSONS
6 COOKING APPLES (1 KG/2 LBS)
1 1/2 TABLESPOONS BROWN SUGAR
1/2 TABLESPOON CINNAMON
1 OR 2 YOGHURTS

1) Wash, peel and core the apples. Cut the apples into small pieces and put them into a saucepan half full of water.

2) Keep the water level in the pan below that of the apples otherwise the apples become soggy. Cook the apples on a medium heat for 20 minutes. Stir in the sugar and cinnamon. Allow excess water to evaporate. Stir and taste occasionally before removing from the heat.

Serve nice and hot, and add the cold yoghurt over the apples which should be mushy.

Preparation time: 35-40 minutes
Cooking time: 55-60 minutes
Standing time: 60 minutes

BASQUE CAKE (***)
"Gâteau Basque"

6 PERSONS
5 EGGS
260 G/ 9 OZ SUGAR (WHITE)
200 G/7 OZ BUTTER
1/4 LITRE/8 FL OZ MILK
325 G/12 OZ FLOUR (WHITE PLAIN)
GRATED RIND OF 1 LEMON
PINCH OF SALT

1) Pour 300 g/11 oz flour into a large mixing bowl and make a hollow in the centre of the flour.
2) Crack open 3 eggs. Pour 2 yolks into the centre of the flour in the bowl. The third egg complete is to be beaten and also poured into the centre. Add 200 g/7 oz sugar into the centre. Add a pinch of salt.
3) Soften 200 g/7 oz butter in a clean saucepan, on a low heat, then add the butter (beginning to melt) to the other ingredients (in the centre) in the mixing bowl. Add the grated rind of one lemon.
4) Slowly blend all the ingredients together with the hands making a thick substance which is then set aside for one hour **.

Pastry Cream "crème pâtissière"

5) Now you have time to prepare your "crème pâtissière". Take 1/4 of a litre/8 fl oz of milk, 2 egg yolks, 60 g/2 oz sugar. and 25 g/1 oz flour. First heat the milk, remove when hot (it should not boil) and transfer to a jug. Place the eggs into the pan on a low heat, add the sugar and flour, and commence stirring, gradually pouring in the hot milk and continuing to stir all the time until you have a cream. It necessary step up the heat. If the liquid becomes lumpy start to beat. Allow the cream to cool.
6) Grease an ovenproof cake dish with 10 g/1 oz butter and a little flour. Pad the sides and bottom of the cake dish with the pastry (4) - best done with the hands again. Pour the cream over the pastry and spread evenly so that the cream covers the pastry. Finally, add the remainder of the pastry on top of the cream so that the cream is now totally covered.
7) Preheat the oven for 10 minutes, and bake for 50 minutes on 170 C/335 F/Gas Mark 3. Remove and allow to cool completely before taking the cake out of the tin; (it is served cold).

Notes: Estimate the size of your cake tin or dish beforehand so that you do not run out of pastry. Best size cake tin would be about 23 cm / 9" in diameter and 6 cm / 2 1/2" high.

** Blend as follows: start by blending the eggs with the butter and sugar, lastly with the flour.

Preparation time: 15-20 minutes
Cooking time: 35-45 minutes

CHOCOLATE CAKE CATALINA (**)

6 TO 8 PERSONS OR MORE
250 G/9 OZ BUTTER
250 G/9 OZ CASTER SUGAR
3 EGGS, BEAT
300 G/11 OZ PLAIN FLOUR
300 /11 OZ CHOCOLATE POWDER
15 G/ 1/2 OZ BAKING-POWDER
1.25 DL/5 FL OZ CREAM
100 G/4 OZ GROUND HAZEL-NUTS

1) Use a large saucepan and melt all the butter using a medium heat.

2) Reduce the heat, add the sugar and stir slowly until the butter and sugar blend, giving a fairly smooth thickish liquid, almost a cream.

3) Beat the eggs and fold into the liquid. Slowly add the flour (to which you have mixed in the baking powder) and continue to stir slowly. Now add the chocolate powder, continue to stir. We now have a thick dark creamy substance which is still sitting over a very low heat. Finally, add the cream and ground hazel-nuts, and continue to stir.

4) In the meantime you will have greased your cake baking tin with a little butter. Pre-heat the oven for 10 minutes, and bake the cake on 180°C/350°F Gas Mark 4 for 30 minutes.

Preparation time: 25-30 minutes
Cooking time: -

CHOCOLATE ICE CREAM (**)

3 TO 4 PERSONS
100 G/1/4 LB PLAIN MILK CHOCOLATE
2 EGGS, SEPARATED
1 1/4 DL/ALMOST 1/4 PINT DOUBLE CREAM
1 TABLESPOON CASTER SUGAR
SLIGHT PINCH OF SALT

1) Separate the eggs and pour the yolks into a fairly large mixing bowl. Add the sugar and a slight pinch of salt. Add the cream and beat together using a whisk (do not whip the cream).

2) Melt the chocolate using a jug or other heat-resistant receptacle. First break the chocolate into small pieces. Place the pieces into a jug. Balance the jug over a saucepan full of hot (not boiling) water until the chocolate has melted (avoid the jug touching the water).
A faster method is to put the chocolate pieces into a heavy-based pan and turn on to a low heat - as the chocolate pieces melt continue to stir - keep the heat low. The risk here is suddenly having the mixture turn lumpy.

3) Transfer the melted chocolate to the mixing bowl (1) and beat again well.

4) Whisk the egg whites until peaks appear and fold gently into the mixture.

5) Finally, place, in a freezer proof container and retain in the freezer until 20 minutes before serving at which time transfer to the refrigerator.

Preparation time: 25-30 minutes

CHOCOLATE & LIME ICE-CREAM (**)

3 TO 4 PERSONS
4 TABLESPOONS CONDENSED MILK, SWEETENED
3 PETITS SUISSES (200 G/8 OZ)
1 DL/4 FL OZ CREAM (TO BE WHIPPED)
100 G/4 OZ PLAIN DARK CHOCOLATE (WITHOUT MILK, WITH SUGAR)
40 G/2 OZ SUGAR
1 EGG, SEPARATED
3 LIMES

1) Mix the condensed milk in a bowl with the petits suisses.

2) Separate the egg yolk from the white. Whisk the egg white until stiff.

3) Whip the cream until nice and thick.

4) Squeeze out the lime juice (from 3 limes) and add to the condensed milk and petits suisses mixture (1) continuing mixing.

5) Melt the chocolate by breaking into small pieces and placing into a heatproof jug or pan and balancing this above a saucepan containing simmering water (the jug or pan should not touch the water otherwise you risk to have lumpy pieces forming).

6) Pour the melted chocolate over the cream (3) and add the egg yolk to this mixture. Now add the condensed milk, all the sugar and petits suisses with lime juice to this same mixture. Continue mixing using a clean wooden spoon.
Finally fold the egg white into the mixture and gently mix again.
Pour the mixture into a receptacle and place in the freezer for 2 hours or more. 30 minutes prior to serving remove and place in the refrigerator..

Note: If you have trouble finding "petits suisses" replace with a light cream cheese such as Mascarpone (use the same quantities for Mascarpone and sweetened condensed milk as indicated above).

Preparation time: 10-15 minutes
Cooking tine: 5-10 minutes

"CRÊME PATISSIÈRE" (*)
Pastry Cream

> 2 TO 4 PERSONS
> 2 EGG YOLKS
> 60 G/2 OZ CASTER SUGAR
> 25 G/1 OZ FLOUR (PLAIN WHITE)
> 1/4 LITRE/8 FL OZ (ALMOST 1/2 PINT) MILK

1) Take 1/4 litre/almost 1/2 pint milk and heat in a clean pan (do not boil). When hot transfer to a jug.

2) Place the egg yolks into a clean saucepan. Use a low heat. Add the sugar and flour. Commence stirring. Gradually pour in the hot milk continuing to stir all the time until you have a cream. If necessary step up the heat very slowly.
If it becomes lumpy remove from the heat and beat.

Note: The key to getting your cream right is really a question of heat control and carefully measuring the ingredients.

For example, during the stirring process you have to increase the heat only slightly, going from simmering to a low boil for one minute, then reduce back to low heat and continue to stir. The cream should be beginning to form, if not, repeat the process of stepping up the heat and reducing quickly. You need lots of patience and time to continue stirring.

Preparation time: 40 minutes
Cooking time: 20 minutes

CREAM SCONES (*)

MAKES 10 TO 12 SCONES
225 G/ 1/2 LB SELF-RAISING FLOUR
75 G/3 OZ FRESH BUTTER
1 TEASPOON BAKING POWDER
40 G/1 1/2 OZ CASTER SUGAR
1 1/2 DL/1/4 PINT MILK
3/4 DL/3 FL OZ CREAM
PINCH OF SALT

1) Sift the flour into a large bowl (using a sieve). Add the baking powder and a slight pinch of salt. Mix in the sugar. Reduce the butter to small pieces and rub into the mixture using your fingertips.

2) Now make a well in the centre of the mixture (1) and pour in the milk. Mix first with a fork. Make another well and pour in the cream. Continue to mix into a light paste this time using your hands (which you first flour to avoid the mixture sticking over all your hands).

3) Spread the paste out onto a board (put flour on the board first). With your hands pat the paste into rounds and cut using a special cutter or sharp knife. Thickness of the rounds should be approximately 1 cm / 1/2". Place the rounds onto a baking sheet or tray (which you have first greased with butter).

4) Pre-heat the oven for 10 minutes. Now bake the scones in the oven for 12 minutes at 200°C/400°F/Gas Mark 6 until the scones have risen and are slightly brown.

At this stage, remove and brush the scones over with a little sweetened milk. Return the scones to the oven for another 5 minutes. Total baking time = 17 minutes, however, avoid over-baking the scones and control carefully.

Preparation time: 20-25 minutes
Cooking, time: 35-45 minutes

CUSTARD FLAN (**)

   3 TO 4 PERSONS
   450 G/1 LB PÂTE À GÂTEAU (PLAIN SHORTCRUST DOUGH)
   10 G/1/2 OZ BUTTER
   2 EGG YOLKS
   60 G/2 OZ CASTER SUGAR
   25 G/1 OZ FLOUR (PLAIN WHITE)
   1/4 LITRE/8 FL OZ (ALMOST 1/2 PINT) MILK
   1/2 TEASPOON VANILLA ESSENCE

1) Roll out the dough (using a little flour so that the dough does not stick) to the size of a flan tin (30 cm approx. in diameter). Remember to grease the tin with a little butter (to prevent sticking). Puncture all the dough in the flat surface of the tin with a fork (to avoid the dough rising with the heat). See note below.

2) Pre-heat your oven for 10 minutes and then bake the dough for 30/40 minutes until a nice light brown colour, on 180°C/350°F/Gas Mark 4.

3) To make the cream, heat the milk in a clean pan (but do not boil). When hot transfer to a jug.

4) Place the egg yolks into a clean saucepan. Use a low heat. Add the sugar and flour. Commence stirring. Gradually pour in the hot milk, continuing to stir. Add the vanilla essence. During the stirring process step up the heat very slowly going gently from simmering to slightly above (very low boil) for one minute, continuing to stir. The cream should be beginning to form, if not, slowly add a little more heat but be ready to reduce quickly. Take your time and stir slowly. Too much heat and lumps start to form. If lumps start forming remove from heat and beat.

5) Allow the cream to cool (the pastry should also be cool) and pour the cream evenly over the open surface of the pastry making the flan.

   Place the flan into the refrigerator until serving.

Note: To avoid the pastry rising in the oven (there is no filling at this stage) you will need to cover the pastry first with grease paper and then set something heavy on the grease paper such as peas or rice (even clean small pebbles or stones will do).

Preparation time: 1 hour
Standing time: 1 hour
plus overnight standing

ENGLISH TRIFLE (**)

4 TO 6 PERSONS
125 G/5 OZ SPONGE FINGERS
50 G/2 OZ MACAROONS
5 TABLESPOONS STRAWBERRY JAM
1 DL/4 FL OZ SHERRY OR MARSALA
1/4 LIT/8 FL OZ CREAM, WHIPPED,
GROUND HAZEL-NUTS, GLACÉ CHERRIES AND/OR OTHER GLACÉ FRUITS
CUSTARD CREAM:
4 EGG YOLKS
60 G/2 1/2 OZ CASTER SUGAR
35 G/1 1/2 OZ FLOUR
1/2 LIT/18 FL OZ MILK, AND VANILLA ESSENCE

1) Each sponge finger should be cut into two halves, covered with jam and pressed together like a sandwich, and halved again.
   The final result will be cubes about 1 to 1 1/2 cm long.
   Press these down to the bottom of a nice large glass bowl.
   Now break the macaroons into small pieces and sprinkle over the sponge fingers. Pour the sherry or marsala over the entire contents and allow to stand for 1 hour.

2) Make your custard cream as follows:
   Heat the milk in a clean pan (but do not boil). When hot transfer to a jug. Place the egg yolks into a clean pan. Use a low heat. Add the sugar and flour. Commence stirring. Gradually pour in the hot milk, continuing to stir. Add the vanilla essence. During the stirring process step up the heat very slowly going gently from simmering to slightly above (very low boil) for one minute, continuing to stir.
   The cream should be beginning to form, if not, slowly add a little more heat but be ready to reduce quickly (see also page 136). Allow the cream to cool and pour over the top of the contents in the bowl.

3) Whip your cream stiffly and pile it on lightly over the top of the custard. Add for decoration glacé cherries and /or other glacé fruits, and ground hazel-nuts. Retain in the refrigerator overnight before serving.

Note: After sprinkling the broken pieces of macaroon over the sponge fingers, and before adding the sherry or Marsala, I recommend using a pestle or something similar so that the ingredients are pressed down tight to the bottom of the bowl.

Preparation time: 10-20 minutes
Cooking time: 5-10 minutes

FRUIT SALAD IN SYRUP (*)

4 PERSONS
150 G/5 OZ GREEN GRAPES
1 MANGO
1 APPLE
1 ORANGE
3 KIWIS
2 BANANAS
2 TANGERINES
4 LIMES
100 G/4 OZ BROWN SUGAR
2 DL/7 FL OZ WATER
1 DL/4 FL OZ WHITE WINE

This is a sample fruit selection; other fruit can be used such as peaches, nectarines, melon, pineapple, etc., depending on the season and availability. The limes and grapes are essential.

1) Wash the limes and grapes. Wash the other fruit and peel as appropriate. Place the grapes into a large serving bowl. Cut the bananas, apples, * oranges and tangerines into small slices and add to the bowl. Peel and add pieces of kiwis. For the mango or similar fruit, peel, cut open and scoop out the flesh and then add to the bowl.

2) Squeeze out the juice from the limes and set aside. Place the rind of the limes (or put the entire remains of the limes after squeezing out the juice) into 2 dl boiling water.
Turn the boiling water back to a simmer and let it remain simmering for 5 minutes. Now strain and keep the liquid (throw the remains of the limes).

3) Place the liquid (2 dl - add more water if necessary) over a low heat. Add the sugar. Stir so that the sugar does not stick to the bottom of the saucepan. When the sugar has dissolved, step up the heat and boil the liquid again for 2 minutes; continue to stir. Remove from the heat and add 1 dl white wine, continuing to stir. Replace on a residual heat for 2 minutes continuing to stir. Pour the syrup into the fruit bowl. Pour in the lime juice, and mix all the syrup with the different fruits.

Retain in the refrigerator until serving.

* Note: First place the small apple slices into water and add lemon juice to avoid the apples discolouring (until your syrup is ready).

Preparation time: 15-20 minutes
Cooking time: 10 minutes

LEMON CREAM (**)

3 TO 4 PERSONS
3 EGGS, SEPARATED
150 G/5 OZ CASTER SUGAR
3 DL/ 1/2 PINT WHIPPING CREAM
JUICE OF 2 LEMONS
RIND OF 1 LEMON, GRATED
2 GLASSES OF COLD WATER

1) Separate the egg yolks from the whites. Pour the yolks together with the sugar into a heavy-based pan. Mix and beat, adding 2 glasses of water. Pour in the juice of 2 lemons. Add the grated rind. Mix and stir.

2) Now turn on the heat and bring to almost boiling (should not boil) continuing to stir. Allow to cool.

3) Whisk the egg whites until stiff (peaks appear). Separately, whip the cream.

4) Firstly, fold in the whipped cream (into the mixture) then fold in the egg whites.

Your lemon cream should be placed into the refrigerator until serving.

Preparation time: 15-20 minutes

LIME CREAM (*)

2 PERSONS
8 TABLESPOONS CONDENSED (SWEETENED) MILK
4 LARGE PETITS SUISSES (APPROX. 200 G/7 OZ)
4 LIMES

1) Thoroughly wash the limes. Grate the lime rind into a saucer.

2) Put the condensed milk and the petits suisses into a mixing bowl and mix them together making a cream.

3) Squeeze the lime juice into the bowl (2) add the lime rind and continue to mix.

Transfer to serving cups, and place in a cool spot until ready for serving.

This dessert is one of my favourites and it is very easy and quick to make.

Preparation time: 20-25 minutes

MOUSSE AU CHOCOLAT (**)

(Chocolate Mousse)

> **4 PERSONS**
> 100 G/4 OZ PLAIN CHOCOLATE
> 1.25 DL/1/4 PINT CREAM (TO BE WHIPPED)
> 1/2 TO 1 TABLESPOON RUM, OR WHISKY
> 2 EGGS, SEPARATED

1) To melt the chocolate, break the chocolate into small pieces, place in a dry heatproof bowl or jug, and position the bowl or jug over a pan of simmering water. Avoid the bowl touching the water (otherwise you risk the chocolate melting and suddenly turning lumpy). Stir with a wooden spoon to help the melting process.
(I usually use two saucepans - a large one with the hot water over the heat, and the second balanced above but not touching the water).

2) Separate the yolks from the whites of the eggs. Add the yolks to the liquid chocolate and mix. Pour in the rum or whisky, and stir and mix well.

3) Whip your cream. Fold the cream into the chocolate mixture. Whisk your egg whites until stiff and also add to the mixture.

4) Mix and stir well again before placing your "mousse au chocolat" into the fridge just to chill - remove from the fridge a good 45 minutes to one hour before serving.

Note: another solution for this recipe, if you have cocoa instead of chocolate, is as follows:

> **50 G/2 OZ COCOA POWDER**
> 75 G/3 OZ BROWN SUGAR
> 2 EGGS, SEPARATED
> 3 TABLESPOONS WATER
> 1/2 TO 1 TABLESPOON RUM, OR WHISKY
> 1.25 DL/ 1/4 PINT CREAM (TO BE WHIPPED)

1) Use a small serving bowl, mix the cocoa in 2 to 3 tablespoons water, add the sugar and mix well.

You then proceed as in steps 2) 3) and 4) above.

Preparation time: 20-30 minutes

RASPBERRY ICE-CREAM (*)

4 PERSONS
300 G/11 OZ RASPBERRIES
120 G/4 OZ CASTER SUGAR
1 TABLESPOON LEMON JUICE
1 EGG YOLK, BEAT FOR 1/2 MINUTE
2 1/2, DL/8 FL OZ DOUBLE CREAM (TO BE WHIPPED FOR NOT MORE THAN 1/2 MINUTE TO MAKE IT THIN AND SLIGHTLY FLOPPY)

1) Pass the raspberries through a fine sieve to obtain a purée.

2) Add the sugar and lemon juice, and mix into the purée.

3) Separately, beat the egg yolk and add to the raspberry mixture. Now mix in the cream and gently continue to mix.

Freeze in a suitable receptacle. Remove from the freezer about 15 minutes before serving.

Preparation time: 30-40 minutes
Cooking time: 40 minutes

ROLY-POLY DESSERT (***)

4 PERSONS
225 G/8 OZ FLOUR
100 G/4 OZ FINELY SHREDDED, BEEF SUET (NOT EASY TO FIND ON THE CONTINENT OF EUROPE)
1 TEASPOON BAKING POWDER
6 TABLESPOONS JAM
1/2 TEASPOON SALT
1 1/2 DL/1/4 PINT MILK
DROP OF WATER FOR BRUSHING THE EDGES OF THE SUET CRUST
A LITTLE BUTTER FOR GREASING THE BAKING TRAY -

1) Mix the flour, suet, baking powder and salt together in a large mixing bowl (large salad bowl will do).

Mix all the ingredients together, first using a fork. Pour in the milk slowly. Continue mixing until you have a stiff paste (best done with your floured hands).

2) Transfer the dough to a lightly floured board. Roll out the dough into a rectangular shape, approx. 1/2 cm/1/4" thick, 24 cm /9 1/2" wide.

Leave a border of 2 1/2 cm/1" down each long edge of the rolled out dough. Now spread the jam evenly over the entire surface of the dough. Roll up the dough tightly, lengthways, similar to a Swiss roll. Seal and secure the sides and edges by brushing with a little water (you do not want the jam to come out during the baking process). When tightly rolled, brush over with a little milk or with the yolk of one egg.

3) Place the pastry on to a baking tray or sheet (previously greased with a little butter). Pre-heat the oven for 10 minutes. Bake for 30 minutes, until a golden brown colour, at 180°C/350°/Gas Mark 4. Serve hot.

Avoid the Roly-Poly becoming too hard and remove from the oven in good time. Five or six tablespoons of jam are a minimum - you need enough jam to cover the entire length of the pastry.

Preparation time: 25-30 minutes

TIRAMISU (***)

2 TO 4 PERSONS (DEPENDING ON HOW YOU LIKE EXCELLENT DESSERTS)
350 G/12 OZ ITALIAN MASCARPONE CHEESE
20 TO 25 SPONGE FINGER BISCUITS
1.25 DL/1 GLASS STRONG COFFEE
5 TABLESPOONS MARSALA
3 EGGS, SEPARATED
3 TABLESPOONS WHITE SUGAR
20 G/1 OZ COCOA POWDER, OR BITTER CHOCOLATE, GRATED
PINCH OF SALT

1) Prepare the coffee and mix with the Marsala. Allow to cool. Place the sponge fingers (break into two parts) into a large serving or mixing bowl. Pour in the coffee and Marsala (after the coffee is cooled). Soak the fingers thoroughly until all the liquid is absorbed. Set aside.

2) Separate the egg yolks from the whites. Whisk the yolks with the sugar, add the Mascarpone. Whisk the egg whites until stiff (add a pinch of salt). Add the whites to the Mascapone mixing gently.

3) Spoon the entire mixture over the sponge fingers. Finally, sprinkle the cocoa powder (or grated chocolate) over the top of the Tiramisu in a very thin layer. Place the Tiramisu in the refrigerator for two to three hours before serving.

Note: The secret is to make sure all the liquid is absorbed by the fingers before adding the other ingredients.

Another solution is to break the sponge fingers into four parts and mash them in the coffee/Marsala liquid at the bottom of the large serving bowl. Wait until all the liquid is absorbed (or almost).

Preparation time: 30-40 minutes

TORINO CHOCOLATE CAKE (***)
(It. Dolce Torino)

> 4 PERSONS
> 200 G/7 OZ MILK CHOCOLATE
> 90 G/3 OZ BUTTER
> 50 G/2 OZ FINE WHITE SUGAR
> 18 TO 20 SPONGE FINGERS
> 1 DL/1/4 PINT KIRSCH
> 1 DL/1/4 PINT CREAM, WHIPPED
> PEELED ALMONDS, GRATED OR CHOPPED

1) Melt the chocolate by breaking into small pieces or grating. Place into a dry heatproof bowl or jug, and position over a pan of simmering water. Avoid the bowl touching the water otherwise you risk the chocolate becoming lumpy. Stir with a clean wooden spoon to help the melting process.
Add the butter and sugar slowly, continuing to stir over a low heat until melted. The end result should be a runny cream.

2) Whip the cream. Mix the cream with the chocolate liquid (1) and stir so that the whipped cream is absorbed. Place the newly made chocolate cream in a cool spot for 5 to 10 minutes (this allows the cream to become more solid for spreading over the sponge fingers).

3) Dip the biscuits (sponge fingers) into the Kirsch. Set the first layer of 6 fingers onto a serving cake dish. Cover these sponge fingers with the chocolate cream (spread evenly using a knife). Proceed evenly in the same manner with the next two layers so that the chocolate cream completely covers the sponge fingers (do not forget to dip the fingers into the Kirsch before setting them on the dish and adding the cream).

4) Add the almonds on top as a decoration, and place the dish into the refrigerator ready for serving (or place into the freezer for 30 to 45 minutes to allow it to settle and become more solid).

Note: After making the chocolate cream if you find it is too liquid you will need to leave it longer in the refrigerator otherwise it becomes difficult to spread over the sponge fingers.
You can also use a freezer-proof rectangular receptacle for the sponge fingers (after they have been dipped in the Kirsch) before pouring on the chocolate cream. Grease the receptacle first to avoiding sticking.

Preparation time: 20-30 minutes
Freezer: 3 to 4 hours

VANILLA ICE CREAM (*)

4 PERSONS
3 EGG YOLKS
2 TEASPOONS VANILLA ESSENCE
1 TABLESPOON CASTER SUGAR
2 1/2 DL / **1/2** PINT DOUBLE CREAM

1) Prepare your egg yolks, vanilla essence and sugar, and beat together in a bowl for approx. one minute. Add 1/2 cup cream, mix, but do not whip.

2) Now whip the remainder of the cream separately (1 1/2 cups). Fold the whipped cream into the bowl with your other ingredients. Mix gently, and transfer the contents to a freezerproof container and place in the freezer for 3 to 4 hours.

3) Remove after one hour and beat, replace in the freezer, and transfer to the refrigerator about 20 minutes before serving.

Preparation time: 30-40 minutes
Cooking time: 15-20 minutes
Standing time: 60 minutes

WILD BERRIES AU GRATIN (***)

(Fr. Gratin aux fruits des bois)

6 TO 8 PERSONS
IT IS PROBABLY UNLIKELY THAT YOU HAVE ACCESS TO WILD STRAWBERRIES AND WILD RASPBERRIES, SO JUST USE FRUIT WHICH ARE IN SEASON -
750 G/ 1 3/4 LBS MIXTURE OF STRAWBERRIES, RASPBERRIES AND BLACKCURRANTS (LARGE STRAWBERRIES SHOULD BE CHOPPED INTO SMALL PARTS)
200 G/8 OZ CASTER SUGAR
2 1/2 DL/ 8 FL OZ (JUST UNDER 1/2 PINT) PASTRY CREAM
2 1/2 DL /8 FL OZ   "   "   "   "   CHANTILLY CREAM
1 DL / 4 FL OZ KIRSCH

For the pastry cream you will need 2 egg yolks, 60 g/2 oz caster sugar, 25 g/1 oz plain white flour. 2 1/2 dl/8 fl oz milk.
for the chantilly cream use 2 1/2 dl/8 fl oz double cream for whipping and 1/2 teaspoon sugar.
You will need small individual, ovenproof pots for the number of servings.

1) Allow the fruit to soak in the sugar for one hour

2) Prepare the chantilly cream simply by whipping the double cream until stiff, adding 1. teaspoon of sugar.

3) For the pastry cream refer to page 134 Allow to cool.

4) Mix the chantilly cream and the pastry cream together adding 1 dl/4 fl oz of Kirsch.

5) Take the number of individual pots needed and fill each one with a portion of the fruit mixture (1). Now cover the top of the fruit with a layer of the cream (4).

6) Pre-heat the grill at maximum for 5 minutes. Place the small pots under the grill at 180°C/350°F/Gas Mark 4 for 3 to 5 minutes until the surface starts to turn brown (you will need to watch carefully so that the surface is not too brown)

Serve quite warm, not too hot.

An abridged version of this recipe was supplied by Stephane RIVASSEAU, Head Chef at the Vereina Hotel at Klosters, Switzerland.

EASY EXCELLENT COOKING GUIDE

GLOSSARY COOKING TERMS AND PROCESSES

BRITISH AND EUROPEAN COOKING AT ITS BEST

GLOSSARY OF COOKING TERMS AND PROCESSES

à la broche	roasted on a spit or skewer -
à la mode de	after the style of, or fashion of -
al dente	used mainly for pasta - not overcooked, just right, slightly resistant, never soggy -
au four	baked in the oven -
au gratin	food cooked in the oven, over which there is a thin light layer of crust (cheese, sauce, etc.) -
bain-marie	a large open vessel, half full with low-boiling water. In the centre is a saucepan containing a liquid (sauce, etc.) which needs to be heated -
bake	to cook by dry heat, as in an oven -
bard	to use a slice of bacon to cover poultry, etc.-
baste	to moisten food which is roasting, with gravy, fat, etc.-
béarnaise	a rich white herb sauce
beat	see whip -
blend	to mix so as to produce a certain quality -
boil	to heat water or any liquid so that bubbles rise continually and break on the surface; water boils at 100°C/212°F (at sea level) -
braise	food is first browned in a small amount of fat in an open pan after which a small quantity of liquid is added, the pan is covered and the food is cooked further -
broil	to cook by direct heat such as meat, fish, etc., cooked on a gridiron over or under a fire - same as grilling -
brown	to partially fry, slightly browning without cooking - "faire revenir" is the French term which is better -
caramelize	to heat sugar to obtain a characteristic flavour -
casserole	a type of stew-pan, and also a dish served in a casserole -

cordon bleu	sometimes used to describe a first-class (female) cook -
dice	to cut into small cubes or squares -
fines-herbes	finely chopped fresh herbs mainly used in egg dishes and sauces -
fritters	fruit, meat, cereal, vegetables or fish covered with batter (or chopped and mixed with batter) usually fried in oil, lard, etc. -
fry	a cooking medium using fat. The quantity of fat (or oil) varies from a small amount in sautéing to a large quantity (covering the food) in deep-frying -
garnish	to complete and decorate a dish prior to serving -
glaze	to treat the food surface to obtain a lacquer-like finish -
grate	to reduce to small particles (as in grated cheese) -
griddle	to cook on a griddle -
grill	to subject meat, fish, etc., to direct, intense heat, as in an oven, placing the food under the grill -
knead	to work dough using the hands, stretching and folding the dough
marinate	to pickle or soak in a liquid (prepare a marinade) -
mijoter	to cook slowly at simmering point -
mince	to finely slice or shred (émincé) -
parboil	to boil until a food is only partially cooked -
pot-roast	the braising of a large piece of meat -
purée	a smooth pulp (mashed vegetables, etc.) obtained by passing ingredients through a sieve -
réduire	to boil liquid gradually to a required consistency, to reduce -
roast	same process of cooking in the oven as in baking, but roasting is usually applied to meats -
roux	a preparation for making a sauce consisting of butter and flour -

sauté	to fry in a pan with little fat or oil over a brisk heat : a sauté-pan is usually a shallow, thin-bottomed frying/cooking pan -
savoury	entremets - food having a stimulating taste or flavour
scald	to heat liquid just short of boiling point -
sear	to remove the redness (from meat) -
season	to add savoury ingredients such as salt and pepper -
simmer	to heat a liquid to just below the boiling point when bubbles form slowly and break below the surface -
steam	to treat with steam for the purpose of heating and cooking -
stew	to cook in a liquid which is boiling slowly (étuvé - étouffée) -
stock	the liquid resulting from the cooking of bones or meat (with or without vegetables or fish) - it is a foundation for soup -
toast	to brown by direct heat -
whip	to beat up into a froth with a fork (eggs, creams, etc.) or other instrument -
whisk	to beat or whip with an implement known as a whisk -

EASY EXCELLENT COOKING GUIDE

INTERNATIONAL VOCABULARY
(ENGLISH, FRENCH AND ITALIAN FOOD NAMES)

BRITISH AND EUROPEAN COOKING AT ITS BEST

International Vocabulary - English, French and Italian

Food Names

English	French	Italian
Soups	**Potages**	**Minestre**
broth	bouillon	brodo
clear soup	consommé	consommé - brodino
onion soup	soupe à l'oignon	zuppa di cipolle
thick soup	purée	purea
Cereals	**Céréales**	**Cereali**
bran	son	crusca
cereal	céréale	cereale
corn	grain de blé	grano
cornflakes	pailletés de maïs	fiocchi di grano
corn-meal	semoule de maïs	semola di mais
dough	pâte	pasta
flour	farine	farina
maize	maïs	grano turco
mealie	maïs	farina di mais
oatmeal	farine d'avoine	farina d'avena
oats	avoine	avena
porridge	bouillie d'avoine	pappa d'avena
rice	riz	riso
rye	seigle	segala
wheat	blé	grano
Wholemeal (bread)	pain complet	pane integrale
yeast	levure	lievito
Pastries and Cakes	**Les Pâtes et Gâteaux**	**Paste, Pasticcerio, Dolci**
batter	pâte à frire	pastella
biscuit	biscuit	biscotto
cake	gâteau	dolce
custard	crème anglaise	crema inglese
doughnut	boule de Berlin	krapfen
dumpling	boulette (de pâte) bouillie	polpetta bollita
flaky, or puff pastry	pâte feuilletée	pasta sfoglia
French crust pastry	pâte brisée	pasta frolla
flan	flan	flan
macaroon	macaron	amaretto
pancake	crêpe	frittella
pastry	pâte, pâtisserie	pasta, pasticceria
pasty	pâté	pasticcino
patty	petit pâté	pasticcio
pie-crust	croûte de pâté	crostata
quiche	quiche	quiche
shortcrust pastry	pâte à gâteau	pasta da focaccia
tart	tarte	torta

English	French	Italian
Game and Poultry	**Gibier et Volaille**	**Selvaggina e Pollame**
capon	chapon	cappone
chicken	poulet	pollo
duck	canard	anitra
duckling	caneton	anitroccolo
fowl	poulet	pollame
game	gibier	Selvaggina
goose	oie	oca
goose liver	foie-gras	fegato d'oca
grouse	coq de bruyère	gallo di montagna
guinea-fowl	pintade	gallina faraona
hare	lièvre	Lepre
partridge	perdrix	pernice
pheasant	faisan	fagiano
pigeon	pigeon	piccione
quail	caille	quaglia
rabbit	lapin	coniglio
snipe	bécassine	beccaccio, beccaccia
turkey	dindon/dinde	tacchino
venison	venaison	cacciagione
widgeon	canard siffleur	folaga (anatra)
woodcock	bécasse	beccaccia
Fish	**Poissons**	**Pesce**
anchovy	anchois	acciuga
angler-fish	baudroie	rana pescatrice
bass, sea bass	bar, loup de mer	spigola
bream	brème, dorade	occhialone, reina
brill	barbue	rombo
carp	carpe	carpa
caviar	caviar	caviale
cod	morue, cabillaud	merluzzo, merluzzetto
crab	crabe	granchio
john dory	saint-pierre	pesce san pietro
eel	anguille	anguilla
flounder	flet, carrelet	pesce passera
haddock	aiglefin	baccalà
hake	merlu - colin	nasello
halibut	flétan	passera
herring	hareng	aringa
kipper	hareng doux	aringa affumicata
lobster	langouste, homard	aragosta
mackerel	maquereau	sgombro
monkfish	ange de mer	squadro

English	French	Italian
mullet, red	rouget	triglia di fanno
mussel	moule	cozza, muscolo
oyster	huître	ostrica
perch	perche	persico
prawn	crevette rose	scampo, gamberetto
pike	brochet	luccio
plaice	plie	passere
salmon	saumon	salmone
sardine	sardine	sardina
scallop	coquille saint-jacques	conchiglia di san jacopo
scampi	scampi	scampi
shrimp	crevette grise	gambero
skate	raie	razza
sole	sole	sogliola
sprat	harenguet	papalina
sturgeon	esturgeon	storione
trout	truite	trota
tuna	thon	tonno
turbot	turbot	rombo chiodato
whitebait	blanchaille	clupea
whiting	merlan	merlano

Vegetables	**Légumes**	**Verdura**
artichoke	artichaut	carciofo
asparagus	asperge	asparago
aubergine/egg-plant	aubergine	melanzane
beans, broad	fèves	fagioli
beans, haricots	Soissons	borlotti
beetroot	betterave	barbabritola
broccoli	broccoli	broccoli
Brussels sprouts	choux de Bruxelles	cavolini di Bruxelles
cabbage	chou	cavolo
capers	câpres	capperi
cardoon	cardon	cardo
carrot	carotte	carota
cauliflower	choufleur	cavofiore
celery	céleri	sedano
cucumber	concombre	cocomero
endive	endive	endivia
fennel	fenouil	finocchio
green peas	pois verts	piselli
horseradish	raifort	cren, rafano
kohlrabi	chou-rave	cavolo rapa
leek	poireau	porro

English	French	Italian
lettuce	laitue	lattuga
lentil	lentille	lenticchia
marrow	courge	zucca
mushroom	champignon	fungo
onion	oignon	cipolla
parsley	persil	prezzemolo
parsnip	panais	pastinaca
peas	petits pois	pisellini
potato	pomme de terre	patata
radish	radis	radicchino
spinach	epinards	spinaci
spring onions	ciboule	cipollina primaverile
swede	chourave de Suède	cavolo navone (di Svezia)
tomato	tomate	pomodoro
turnip	navet (rave)	rapa
watercress	cresson	radicchio
vegetables	légumes	verdura/legumi
zucchini	courgettes	zucchini

Spices	**Epices**	**Spezie**
allspice	piment	pimento
caper	câpre	cappero
caraway	carvi	carvi
cardamom	cardamome	cardamomo
cayenne	cayenne	pepe di Calenna
chilli	poivre de Guinée	pepe di Guaiana
cinnamon	cannelle	cannella
clove	clou de girofle	chiodo di garofano
coriander	coriandre	coriandro
cumin	cumin	kümmel
curry powder	cari	polvere di curry
ginger	gingembre	zenzero
juniper	genièvre	ginepro
mace	fleur de muscade	fiore moscato
nutmeg	noix de muscade	noce moscata
paprika	paprika	paprica
pepper	poivre	pepe
saffron	safran	zafferano
turmeric	curcuma	cumarina
vanilla	vanille	vaniglia

Herbs	**Herbes**	**Erbaggi (Erbe)**
basil	basilic	basilico
bayleaf (laurel)	laurier	lauro (foglie di)

English	French	Italian
borage	bourrache	borraggine
bouquet garni	bouquet garni	erbaggi misti
chervil	cerfeuil	caprifoglio
chives	ciboulette	cipollina
dill	aneth	aneto
eschalot	échalote	cipollina
fennel	fenouil	finocchio
garlic	ail	aglio
clove of garlic	gousse d'ail	spicchio d'aglio
marjoram	marjolaine	maggiorana
mint	menthe	menta
oregano	origan	origano
parsley	persil	prezzemolo
rosemary	romarin	rosmarino
sage	sauge	salvia
savory	sarriette	santoreggia, satureia
tarragon	estragon	dragoncello
thyme	thym	timo

Meat	**Viande**	**Carne**
bacon	lard	lardo
beef	boeuf	bue
brain	cervelle	cervella
breast	poitrine	petto
cutlet - chop	côtelette	cotolette - costa
fillet	filet	filetto
joint	morceau	pezzo
kidney	rognon	rognone
lamb	agneau	agnello
leg	gigot	cosciotto (di agnello)
liver	foie	fegato
loin	longe	lombata
mutton	mouton	montone
neck	cou	collo
offal	abats	frattaglie
pork	porc	maiale
rib	côte	costola
rump	culotte	brache
saddle	selle	sella
sausage	saucisse	salsiccia, salame
shoulder	épaule	spalla
sirloin	aloyau	dorso di bue
slice	tranche	fetta
steak	bifteck	bistecca

English	French	Italian
stew	ragoût (étuvé - étouffé)	stufato, stufatino
stuffing	farce	ripieno
sweetbreads	ris de veau	animelle
tongue	langue	lingua
trotter	pied de porc	piedino di maiale
veal	veau	vitello - vitella
venison	venaison	salvaggina

Dairy Products	**Produits Laitiers**	**Latticini**
butter	beurre	burro
cheese	fromage	formaggio
condensed milk	lait condensé	latte condensato
cream	crème	panna
milk	lait	latte
ricotta	ricotta (serré)	ricotta
skim milk	lait écrémé	latte seremato
yoghurt (yoghurt)	yahourt	yogurt

Fruit	**Fruits**	**Frutta**
apple	pomme	mela
apricot	abricot	albicocca
avocado	avocat	avocado
banana	banane	banana
blackberry	mûre	mora
blackcurrant	cassis	ribes nero
cherry	cerise	ciliegia
chestnut	marron	castagna
coconut	noix de coco	noce di cocco
damson	prune de damas	prugna di Damasco
date	datte	dattero
fig	figue	fico
gooseberry	groseille	ribes
grape	raisins	uva
grapefruit	grapefruit	pompelmo
greengage	prune	susina
hazelnut	noisette	nocciola
lemon	citron	limone
lime juice	jus de limette	sugo di limettina
mango	mangue	mango
melon	melon	melone, popone
mulberry	mûre	mora
nectarine	nectarine	nettarina
nut	noix	noce
olive	olive	oliva

English	French	Italian
orange	orange	arancia
peach	pêche	pesca
pear	poire	pera
pineapple	ananas	ananas
plum	pruneau	prugna
pomegranate	grenade	melagrana
quince	coing	cotogna
raspberry	framboise	lampone
redcurrant	groseille rouge	ribes rosso
rhubarb	rhubarbe	rabarbaro
strawberry	fraise	fragola
tangerine	manderine	mandarino
walnut	noix	noce

EASY EXCELLENT COOKING GUIDE

HOW TO COOK PASTA

BRITISH AND EUROPEAN COOKING AT ITS BEST

COOKING PASTA

HOW MANY TYPES OF PASTA

There seems to be no limit to the different kinds of Italian Pasta. Different names exist for the same kinds of Pasta, which also helps to complicate the Pasta scene.

HOW TO COOK PASTA

Cook in a large saucepan, filled with salted water (count approximately 1 litre of water to 100 g of Pasta, and 1 to 1 1/2 teaspoons of salt to 1 to 1 1/2 litres of water).

Add the Pasta to the water as soon as the water boils. Stir the Pasta with a fork so that it does not stick together.

Adding oil also helps the non-sticking process (1 tablespoon oil) particularly with spaghetti and long macaronni.

Now place the lid on the pan until the water comes to the boil again, then remove the lid and keep it off during the entire cooking. The water must always be boiling. Never overcook Pasta, and make sure to taste it to achieve the "al dente" refinement stage (which means, just right, slightly resistant, never soggy). At this moment, immediately remove the pan from the heat, drain off the water, retaining a little water in case you need to moisten the Pasta later. Some schools suggest washing the Pasta at this stage with hot water to remove the starch.

Place the Pasta back into the hot saucepan until ready for serving. Add 10 g of butter to the hot Pasta (or 20 g for more servings) to moisten the Pasta even more. When preparing a sauce, as soon as it is ready, empty the Pasta into the sauce and mix thoroughly; in this way you do not lose any part of the sauce. If you have a small quantity of sauce and lots of Pasta you have to reverse the operation and empty the sauce into the Pasta pan.

Serve direct from the recipient containing the Pasta and sauce. Serve on hot plates if possible, and if appropriate add grated cheese, to taste, usually Parmesan. Grated cheese is not required with certain sauces.

EASY EXCELLENT COOKING GUIDE

INDEX
ALL RECIPES IN ALPHABETICAL ORDER

BRITISH AND EUROPEAN COOKING AT ITS BEST

EASY EXCELLENT COOKING GUIDE
Index with page numbers

—A—   Page
APPLE & YOGURT   (*)   129
APPLE CRUMBLE   (**)   127
APPLE TART   (*)   128
ARTICHOKE OMELETTE   (**)   25
ARTICHOKES "PROVENCALE"   (**)   77
ASPARAGUS & BROCCOLI SALAD   (*)   59
AVOCADO WITH PARMA HAM   (*)   60

—B—
BAKED MASHED POTATOES & MINCED BEEF   (***)   95
BAKED POTATOES   (*)   87
BASQUE CAKE   (***)   130
BECHAMEL SAUCE   (*)   20
BEEF & MORTADELLA HAMBURGERS   (*)   96
BEEF STEAKS WITH "HERBES DE PROVENCE"   (*)   97
BELCAMPO SAUCE FOR PASTA   (***)   42
BOILED POTATOES   (*)   87
BOLOGNESE SAUCE   (***)   44
BROCCOBURGERS   (**)   98
BROCCOLI FLAN   (*)   86

—C—
CAPRICCIOSA SALAD   (*)   61
CAULIFLOWER & CHEESE SAVOURY   (**)   90
CAULIFLOWER AU GRATIN   (***)   78
CELERY, BACON AND CHEESE CLANGER   (***)   85
CELERY SOUP   (**)   3
CHEESE & EGG RELISH   (*)   22
CHEESE BISCUITS   (**)   21
CHEESE OMELETTE WITH PARSLEY   (*)   26
CHEESE RECIPES   13-22
   BECHAMEL SAUCE   (*)   20
   CHEESE & EGG RELISH   (*)   22
   CHEESE BISCUITS   (**)   21

CHEESE ON TOAST WITH BACON OR HAM	(*)	15
SAVOURY CHEESE FLAN	(***)	12
SAVOURY TOMATOES WITH CHEESE	(**)	16
SOUFFLE AU FROMAGE	(***)	18
WELSH RABBIT OR RAREBIT	(**)	19
CHEESE SOUFFLE	(***)	18
CHICKEN LIVER PATE	(***)	111
CHICKEN LIVERS WITH MARSALA	(**)	110
CHOCOLATE & LIME ICE-CREAM	(**)	133
CHOCOLATE CAKE CATALINA	(**)	131
CHOCOLATE ICE CREAM	(**)	132
CHOCOLATE MOUSSE	(**)	141
CORNISH PASTIES	(***)	99
COURGETTE OMELETTE	(**)	27
COURGETTES & CAULIFLOWER SALAD	(*)	62
CREAM SCONES	(*)	135
CREME PATISSIERE	(*)	134
CROSTINI DI FEGATINI	(***)	111
CROUTE AU FROMAGE AVEC LARD OU JAMBON	(*)	15
CUSTARD FLAN	(**)	136

—D—

DESSERT RECIPES		125-147
APPLE & YOGURT	(*)	129
APPLE CRUMBLE	(**)	127
APPLE TART	(*)	128
BASQUE CAKE	(***)	130
CHOCOLATE & LIME ICE CREAM	(**)	133
CHOCOLATE CAKE CATALINA	(**)	131
CHOCOLATE ICE-CREAM	(**)	132
CREAM SCONES	(*)	135
CRÊME PATISSIÈRE	(*)	134
CUSTARD FLAN	(**)	136
ENGLISH TRIFLE	(**)	137
FRUIT SALAD IN SYRUP	(*)	138
LEMON CREAM	(**)	139
LIME CREAM	(*)	140
MOUSSE AU CHOCOLAT	(**)	141

PASTRY CREAM	(*)	134
RASPBERRY ICE-CREAM	(*)	142
ROLY-POLY DESSERT	(***)	143
TIRAMISU	(***)	144
TORINO CHOCOLATE CAKE	(***)	145
VANILLA ICE CREAM	(*)	146
WILD BERRIES AU GRATIN	(***)	147
DOLCE TORINO	(***)	145

—E—

EGGS A LA FLORENTINE	(**)	31
EGGS RECIPES		23-31
EGGS A LA FLORENTINE	(**)	31
OMELETTE ARTICHOKES	(**)	25
OMELETTE WITH CHEESE & PARSLEY	(*)	26
OMELETTE WITH COURGETTES	(**)	27
PANCAKES WITH SUGAR & LEMON	(*)	28
SCRAMBLED EGGS (XF)	(*)	29
SCRAMBLED EGGS, MUSHROOMS, ONIONS & CHEESE	(**)	30
ENGLISH TRIFLE	(**)	137

—F—

FENNEL SALAD	(*)	63
FENNEL SOUP	(**)	4
FENNELS AU GRATIN	(***)	79
FENNELS WITH WHITE WINE	(**)	80
FILLETS OF PERCH	(**)	117
FILLETS OF SOLE	(**)	120
FISH RECIPES		113-123
FILLETS OF SOLE	(**)	120
GRILLED SALMON	(**)	119
GRILLED SOLE WITH TOMATOES	(**)	123
PAN-BAKED TROUT	(**)	116
PERCH FILLETS	(**)	117
RED MULLET GRILLED	(**)	118
SEA BASS, BAKED IN THE OVEN	(**)	115
SOLE BAKED IN THE OVEN	(**)	122

TROUT IN OLIVE OIL	(*)	121
FLORENTINE HAMBURGERS	(**)	100
FRENCH BEANS IN SALAD	(*)	64
FRUIT SALAD IN SYRUP	(*)	138

—G—

GARLIC SOUP	(*)	5
GÂTEAU BASQUE	(***)	130
GAZPACHO	(*)	12
GLOSSARY		149-153
GRATIN DE MACARONI	(**)	36
GREEN PEA SOUP	(*)	6
GREEN RICE	(**)	49
GREEN SALAD WITH DRESSING	(*)	65
GRILLED MULLET	(**)	118
GRILLED SALMON WITH HERBS	(**)	119
GRILLED SOLE WITH TOMATOES	(**)	123
GUINEA FOWL, ROASTED	(**)	112

—H—

HAMBURGERS		96-100
BEEF & MORTADELLA	(*)	96
BROCCOBURGERS	(**)	98
FLORENTINE	(**)	100
HOW TO COOK PASTA		165-167

—I—

IRISH STEW	(***)	101
ITALIAN CHOCOLATE CAKE	(***)	145
ITALO-LYONNAISE SALAD	(*)	66

—K—

KOHLRABI SALAD	(*)	67

—L—

LANCASHIRE HOT-POT	(***)	102
LEMON CREAM	(**)	139
LENTIL SALAD	(*)	68
LENTIL SOUP	(*)	7
LIME CREAM	(*)	140

—M—

MACARONI AL PESTO	(*)	37
MACARONI AU GRATIN	(**)	36-37
MACARONI BELCAMPO	(**)	35
MASHED POTATOES WITH SAUSAGES & ONIONS	(**)	88
MEAT & POULTRY RECIPES		93-112
BAKED MASHED POTATOES WITH MINCED BEEF	(***)	95
BEEF & MORTADELLA HAMBURGERS	(*)	96
BEEF STEAKS WITH "HERBES DE PROVENCE"	(*)	97
BROCCOBURGERS	(**)	98
CHICKEN LIVER PATE	(***)	111
CHICKEN LIVERS W/ MARSALA	(**)	110
CORNISH PASTIES	(***)	99
FLORENTINE HAMBURGERS	(**)	100
GUINEA FOWL, ROASTED	(**)	112
IRISH STEW	(***)	101
LANCASHIRE HOT-POT	(***)	102
MOUSSAKA	(**)	103
ROAST PORK WITH HERBS	(***)	104
STEAK & KIDNEY PIE	(***)	105
SWISS SHEPHERD'S PIE	(***)	106
TOURNEDOS EN CROUTE	(***)	107
VEAL CUTLETS WITH MARSALA	(**)	108
VEAL STEW A LA PARISIENNE	(***)	109
MINESTRONE	(***)	8
MOUSSAKA	(**)	103
MOUSSE AU CHOCOLAT	(**)	139
MOZZARELLA & TOMATO SALAD (XF)	(*)	69
MULLET, RED, GRILLED	(**)	118

—N—
NIÇOISE SALAD (**) 70

—O—
OMELETTE WITH ARTICHOKES (**) 25
OMELETTE WITH CHEESE & PARSLEY (*) 26
OMELETTE WITH COURGETTES (**) 27

—P—
PAN-BAKED TROUT (**) 116
PANCAKES WITH SUGAR & LEMON (*) 28
PASTA RECIPES 33-46
   BELCAMPO SAUCE FOR PASTA (***) 42
   BOLOGNESE SAUCE (***) 44
   MACARONI AL PESTO (*) 37
   MACARONI BELCAMPO (**) 35
   MACARONI GRATIN (**) 36
   PASTA WITH PEPPERS (**) 38
   PESTO SAUCE (**) 43
   SPAGHETTI WITH BELCAMPO SAUCE (***) 39
   SPAGHETTI WITH PESTO (*) 40
   TAGLIATELLE WITH TOMATOES, ANCHOVIES OLIVES, BASIL
(**) 41
PASTA WITH PEPPERS & ANCHOVIES (**) 38
PASTRY CREAM (*) 134
PEPPERS WITH ANCHOVIES (*) 81
PEPPERS WITH SAVOURY STUFFING (***) 84
PERCH FILLETS (**) 117
PESTO SAUCE (**) 43
PETITS FOIES DE VOLAILLES AU MARSALA (**) 110
PIPERADE (***) 82
PIZZA (**) 45
PIZZA TO-MO (**) 46
POLENTA WITH CHEESE (**) 55
POLPETTINE ALLA FIORENTINA (**) 100
POTATOES BAKED/BOILED/ROASTED (*) 87
POTATOES, SAUSAGES & ONIONS (**) 88

—R—

RASPBERRY ICE-CREAM	(*)	142
RED MULLET, GRILLED	(**)	118
RICE JARDINIERE	(**)	51
RICE SALAD	(**)	52
RICE WITH ASPARAGUS	(***)	50
RISOTTO MILANESE	(***)	53
RIZ GITANE	(**)	54
ROAST PORK WITH HERBS	(***)	104
ROAST POTATOES	(*)	87
ROLY-POLY DESSERT	(***)	143
RÖSTI	(**)	89

—S—

SALAD RECIPES			57-74
ASPARAGUS & BROCCOLI		(*)	59
AVOCADO WITH PARMA HAM		(*)	60
CAPRICCIOSA		(*)	61
COURGETTES & CAULIFLOWER		(*)	62
FENNEL		(*)	63
FRENCH BEANS		(*)	64
GREEN SALAD WITH DRESSING		(*)	65
ITALO-LYONNAISE		(*)	66
KOHLRABI		(*)	67
LENTIL		(*)	68
MOZZARELLA	(XF)	(*)	69
NIÇOISE		(**)	70
RICE		(**)	52
SPANISH SUMMER SALAD		(*)	74
SPECIAL DRESSING		(*)	73
SPINACH & AVOCADO		(*)	71
SPINACH		(*)	72
VINAIGRETTE DRESSING		(*)	73
WHIMSICAL		(*)	61
SALADE NICOISE		(**)	70
SALMON, GRILLED W/ HERBS		(**)	119
SAVOURY CHEESE FLAN		(***)	16
SAVOURY GREEN BEANS		(**)	91

SAVOURY TOMATOES WITH CHEESE		(**)	17
SCRAMBLED EGGS	(XF)	(*)	29
SCRAMBLED EGGS, MUSHROOMS, ONIONS & CHEESE		(**)	30
SEA BASS, BAKED IN THE OVEN		(**)	115
SOLE BAKED IN THE OVEN		(**)	122
SOLE FILLETS		(**)	120
SOUFFLE AU FROMAGE		(***)	18
SOUP RECIPES			1-12
CELERY		(**)	3
FENNEL		(**)	4
GARLIC		(*)	5
GAZPACHO		(*)	12
GREEN PEA		(*)	6
LENTIL		(*)	7
MINESTRONE		(***)	8
THICK TOMATO	(XF)	(*)	9
TOMATO		(*)	10
VEGETABLE		(**)	11
SPAGHETTI WITH BELCAMPO SAUCE		(***)	39
SPAGHETTI WITH PESTO SAUCE		(*)	40
SPANISH SUMMER SALAD		(*)	74
SPECIAL SALAD DRESSING		(*)	73
SPINACH & AVOCADO SALAD		(*)	71
SPINACH & SAGE		(*)	83
SPINACH SALAD		(*)	72
STEAK & KIDNEY PIE		(***)	105
STUFFED POM-POMS		(***)	84
SWISS SHEPHERD'S PIE		(***)	106

—T—

TAGLIATELLE WITH TOMATOES, OLIVES, ANCHOVIES, BASIL		(**)	41
THICK TOMATO SOUP	(XF)	(*)	9
TIRAMISU		(***)	144
TOMATO SOUP		(*)	10
TO-MO-PIZZA		(**)	46
TORINO CHOCOLATE CAKE		(***)	145
TOURNEDOS EN CROUTE		(***)	107
TROUT IN OLIVE OIL		(*)	121
TROUT, PAN-BAKED		(**)	116

—V—

VANILLA ICE CREAM	(*)	146
VEAL CUTLETS WITH MARSALA	(**)	108
VEAL STEW A LA PARISIENNE	(***)	109
VEGETABLE RECIPES		75-91
ARTICHOKES PROVENCALE	(**)	77
BROCCOLI FLAN	(*)	86
CAULIFLOWER & CHEESE SAVOURY	(**)	90
CAULIFLOWER AU GRATIN	(***)	78
CELERY, BACON AND CHEESE CLANGER	(***)	85
FENNELS AU GRATIN	(***)	79
FENNELS WITH WHITE WINE	(**)	80
PEPPERS WITH ANCHOVIES	(*)	81
PIPERADE	(***)	82
POTATOE DISHES		87-89
BAKED/BOILED/ROASTED	(*)	87
MASHED POTATOES W/ ONIONS & SAUSAGES	(**)	88
RÖSTI	(**)	89
SAVOURY GREEN BEANS	(**)	91
SPINACH & SAGE	(*)	83
STUFFED POM-POMS	(***)	84
VEGETABLE SOUP	(**)	11
VINAIGRETTE SALAD DRESSING	(*)	73
VOCABULARY		155-163

—W—

WELSH RABBIT (RAREBIT)	(**)	19
WHIMSICAL SALAD	(*)	61
WILD BERRIES AU GRATIN	(***)	147

Notes:
* = Simple
** = Not difficult
*** = Slightly more advanced
(XF) = fast